GREAT
SCRAPBOOKS

▲ *HUGS, LOVE, AND KISSES, by Kristi Hazelrigg and Angi Watters, Seminole, OK.*

MEMORY MAKERS®

GREAT SCRAPBOOKS

Ideas, Tips & Techniques

MICHELE GERBRANDT AND
JUDITH DURANT

BARNES & NOBLE BOOKS

NEW YORK

This edition published by Barnes & Noble Inc.
by arrangement with Hugh Lauter Levin Associates, Inc.

2004 Barnes & Noble Books

© 2000 Hugh Lauter Levin Associates, Inc.
http://www.HLLA.com

ISBN: 0-7607-5645-7
M 10 9 8 7 6 5 4 3 2 1

Project Director/Editor: Leslie Conron Carola
Design: Kathleen Herlihy-Paoli
Copy Editor: Deborah Teipel Zindell

The page ideas featured are from the readers and artists of
Memory Makers ® scrapbook magazine, published by:
F and W Publications
12365 North Huron, Suite 500
Denver, CO 80234-3438
www.memorymakersmagazine.com

Idea Coordinator: Pennie Stutzman
Craft Coordinator: Pam Klassen
Photo Directors: Ron Gerbrandt and Linda Flemming
Photo Studios: Jim Cambon and Carol Conway
Photo Production: Diane Gibbs

Originally co-published by F and W Publications and
Hugh Lauter Levin Associates, Inc.

Printed in Hong Kong

CONTENTS

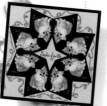

Mackenzie helping
Aunt Vivie make
brownies.
She was a lot
of help and had so
much fun.

MILK

Mackenzie 4 yr.

8/98

INTRODUCTION

What to do with a visiting niece on a late afternoon? Everybody loves brownies. Why not make a batch or two? And, in the process, make a friend for life. MacKenzie's mother took this brownie baking an enticing step forward by taking delightful photographs—and then creating a charming scrapbook page for MacKenzie to cherish forever. (Mother and aunt will cherish it as well.) And, who knows, we may have witnessed the first step in the development of a future pastry chef!

The ideas for creating a scrapbook can come from many sources. In this case, what to do on what might have been a boring afternoon became the driving force for an activity which a mother opted to preserve and remember—a child helping her aunt make brownies. No child could resist that offer, and no one could resist MacKenzie's 100-watt smile as she licks and stirs and licks! This is what childhood is all about. And this is just what scrapbooking is all about—savoring and then preserving life's moments—large and small, life-changing and life-affirming.

All families deserve to have their treasured memories kept alive, and certainly every family has more than enough stories to make an interesting book.

We all have stories to tell—simply by being alive. The stories are special because they are ours. And it is the collection of our stories that brings form and focus to our memories.

No wonder we love to scrapbook.

◀ *MACKENZIE MAKES BROWNIES, by Veronica Gomes, Willows, CA. The images of MacKenzie, a baker at work, with brownie batter all over her hands and face will bring a smile to anyone's face for a long time. The simple page uses baking-theme stickers as decorative elements surrounding the bold single-theme photos of MacKenzie. The soft, rounded corners on the photos and mats and the homespun "stitched" lines add a nice touch. The written information completes the page with the date, MacKenzie's age, and the activity.*

For centuries we have taken pleasure in the handwork of crafts. The instinct to create a book of memories is strong. And the pride that many women and men (yes, men *do* scrapbook) take in creating beautiful handmade objects for their homes is tremendous.

Much more than the sum of its parts, a great scrapbook page is a work of art. *Great Scrapbooks: Ideas, Tips & Techniques* offers the opportunity to learn the art of the craft from the best scrapbookers around the country—scrapbookers who take pride as well as pleasure in the pages they turn out for their families.

Many of our favorite pages have been created using special techniques. They are included here (at least one per chapter) with step-by-step process photos and easy-to-follow instructions. Lift-the-flaps, pop-ups, mosaics, pierced paper, punched paper, pieced paper, kaleidoscopes, die cuts, templates— you'll find them all here, with ideas on how and when to use them.

Keep treasured family memories alive. Dip into that box of old photos, or shoot some new pictures, and tell *your* family story in your own way.

▲ *Sweet Dreams, by Anna Walton, Barnhart, MO.*

Photo: Charlotte Wilhite, Fort Worth, TX

GETTING ORGANIZED

Rummaging through that old box of photos and reminiscing about the "good ol' days" is only the beginning of scrapbooking fun. But where do you start? The answer is, anywhere. You may simply choose a few photos and get right to it. But if you want to make sure you don't miss anything, start by organizing your photos.

Make a work area, gather a few essentials (a pen, stickie notes, etc.), decide on a type of album (either ongoing or specific), create categories and sort your photos within them. Be sure to store the photos in a safe environment.

▲ DADDY'S CASTLE, by Beth Ortstadt, Wichita, KS. Through the arched windows of a detailed reconstruction of a medieval castle we glimpse a father and child at play. Strong geometric shapes and a simple palette present the perfect backdrop for charming images.

THE TOOLS

Albums come in a variety of shapes and styles, including post-bound, three-ring binder, and strap-style, all of which allow you to remove, add, or rearrange pages for ongoing projects. Spiral-bound albums are great for recording a special event or for gift giving. The quantity and size of your photos will help determine the size of the album you need. Make sure that the album you choose provides an acid-free, safe environment for your photos.

Decorative papers are available in a wide variety of eye-catching colors and patterns. Look for papers that are acid- and lignin-free to prevent fading or other damage to your photos. Papers are very versatile—use them to mat or frame photos, as an accent to your scrapbook page, or as a background for an entire page.

Use templates to shape paper or crop photos. Templates help you turn ordinary rectangular photos into whimsical shapes, cut decorative mats to enhance your photos, or create custom-made die cuts.

▲ *PLAYTIME AT THE PARK, by Pam Klassen, Denver, CO. Photographs by Elizabeth Wallis.*

Decorative scissors create unique edges on photos and papers. From elegant scallops to deckle-edged designs, there's a wide variety of patterns available. You'll also need a pair of sharp straight-edged scissors.

Look for glues, tapes, and mounting corners that are labeled "acid-free" and "photo-safe." Rubber cement, white glue, and cellophane tape contain chemicals that may adversely affect photos over time.

Journaling adds a voice as well as pertinent facts to a scrapbook. Journaling pens are available in a rainbow of colors, and a variety of pen tips makes fancy penmanship a breeze. Pigment ink pens are permanent, and your words won't fade like unrecorded memories.

STARTING A PROJECT

Armed with photos, album, and tools, you're ready to make your first page. Know what you want to accomplish and plan it out carefully before cropping any photos or affixing anything to the page.

1. CROPPING

Cropping your photos allows you to enhance the image by eliminating extraneous portions of the shot or by turning it into a unique shape. Create shaped photos by tracing around a template. Or create a silhouette by carefully cutting out the photo's subject and discarding the background. Before trimming, ask yourself if this portion of the photo adds interest, mood, or balance. Does it help date or place the subject? Taken out of context, can the image stand alone?

2. MATTING

Matting photos prior to mounting can help focus attention on the photos and add visual interest and balance to a page. Mat a cropped photo by adhering it to a piece of acid-free paper. Cover these with a template that is slightly larger than the photo. Trace around the template and cut. Or cut the mat freehand. For added dimension, make several layers of mats, each slightly larger than the previous one.

3. MOUNTING

It is not terribly tricky to mount photos in your album. Double-sided tapes and liquid adhesives create a permanent bond. Photo corners are paper or plastic triangles that are applied to the album page—photos are then slipped into the triangles. This allows you to place and easily remove photos from the album. Photo corners come in different sizes, shapes, and styles, from plain to fancy.

4. JOURNALING

Next to your photos, there is nothing more valuable than the information written about them. Who or what is that? Where are we? How long ago was this? These are the details that will disappear from memory over time if they aren't included in your scrapbook. Some subjective comments are also effective. What is being celebrated? What are your feelings about the event? Or place the event in a context. Each page has its own personality and its own reason for being part of your book.

Kaila, Alex, and Kylie had so much fun posing for these pictures in November 1998. Each of the girls received two of these pictures in frames as Christmas gifts. They were a big hit!

Kylie

Kaila

Alex

Best of

Friends

DESIGNING THE PAGE

Now that you know the basics, keeping these simple design ideas in mind will help you create scrapbook pages that are pleasing to the eye and the heart.

❖ *KEEP A FOCAL POINT.* The focal point is the primary image or area on the page—it's where the eye looks first. It may be a centrally located photo, a photo that is larger than the others on a page, a unique or exceptional photo, or a photo that is matted with a special paper or technique that makes it stand out from the others. Supporting images elaborate the main photo or theme. They may be smaller than the main photo and either depict the same scene or time as the primary shot or provide extra information.

❖ *CREATE BALANCE.* Large, bright, and busy photos feel heavier than their counterparts. Place your selected photos on the page and move them around until the page is balanced, that is, no one area overpowers the others. If you are creating a two-page spread, make sure the pages don't appear lopsided.

❖ *ADD COLOR.* Color sets mood, provides balance, and illuminates the photos on your page. Choose colors for background, mats, and accents that convey the feelings of the photos and the events they record. When it comes to color, less is sometimes more. Too much color can be a distraction.

With these basic techniques, there is no limit to the types and styles of scrapbook pages you can create. Remember to keep it simple when you start out; you don't have to fill the page with images.

◄ BEST OF FRIENDS, *by Tara Schneider, Virginia Beach, VA. Strong shapes dominate these cheerful pages. Photos are cropped, matted, and mounted in basic geometric shapes—the photos themselves dictated the cropped shape. The double matting (purple and then white) defines the images and draws the eye to the girls' happy faces. The photos can be cropped with commercial templates or with your own handmade templates once you've decided which parts of the photos you want to include on the scrapbook page.*

► CHRISTMAS LIGHTS, *by Joy Carey, Visalia, CA. Photos are matted with colored paper and cut with decorative-edged scissors. Using a light box, trace light bulbs onto white paper and color them with watercolors and black pen. Arrange and mount on the page as shown. Journal, label, and decorate the page with white pen.*

We presented three scrapbook artists with the same materials and instructions and waited to see the results. Each was given photos of Alexandra Nicole (photos by Erica Pierovich); three printed papers—floral, plaid, and squiggle; two colors of cardstock—yellow and blue. Instructions were minimal: Create a spring page using these photos, at least two of the papers, and any techniques and tools desired.

What better way to celebrate a spring day? Donna W. Pittard of Kingwood, Texas, created a coherent, dynamic design image (*opposite page*) that captures the essence of spring. Photos closely cropped in interesting shapes form a butterfly's outstretched wings, and the plaid paper is trimmed to mat the photos. The body of the butterfly was cut from cardstock and squiggle paper, and the antennae were created with circular journaling. Donna used an embossing stylus, decorating chalk, and cosmetic brushes (to apply the chalk) in addition to the materials provided.

Terri Robichon of Plymouth, Minnesota, cropped her photos to sizes and shapes that accentuate the subject (*below right*). She matted two of the photos with the squiggle paper and arranged all on the floral paper. Using a letter stencil, she created the page title using cardstock, then added journaling with a pen.

Joy Carey of Visalia, California, added watercolor flowers to her page (*below left*)—the line art is adapted from the book, *Eliza Jane Originals: Welcome the Seasons* by Marie Cole. Joy cut strips of plaid paper and applied them as borders. The photos and title are matted with the squiggle paper, and the photos are applied to the mats with photo corners. All decorative lettering was done by hand.

TIP: BASIC CROPPING

❖ *Let the images dictate the cropping.* What is important in the photo? Why are you including it here? Where do you want the eye to focus?

❖ *Shape adds interest to a page.* Don't feel limited by the shape of the original photo. Experiment. Different themes are supported by the shapes of the images as well as by the decorative details.

▲ Rollin' Rollin' Rollin', *by Eve Lowey, Huntington Beach, CA.* *A wonderful series of action photos was taken as baby Jared was* *rolling over. The first shot sets the tone. Silhouetted remaining shots* *are overlapped to give the feeling of motion.*

FAMILY

PAGES

BABIES

Hands down, baby books are the most popular album themes at *Memory Makers* magazine. Requests for baby book scrapbook page ideas outnumber every other category by 4 to 1. Is it any wonder? How else can parents and grandparents and aunts and uncles celebrate this awe-inspiring event? There really is nothing that pulls a family closer together than the celebration of the birth of a child. What hope, what faith in the future, what trust! And all of it deserves to be celebrated and honored in the best way we know how. Creating a memory book to be cherished by generations of family members is an appropriate and loving celebration gift for the new being. Many people who may never have considered scrapbooking do so when a baby is born into their lives.

As with any scrapbook, a baby album requires both a plan and photos. One of the nicest aspects of scrapbooking is the opportunity it presents to include ideas and techniques from other crafts. Quilting has always been an important craft, and quilt patterns are a popular motif with scrapbookers. What you can do with fabric you can do with paper. Quilt patterns can be adapted to create beautiful frames, borders, or even the central motif on a large page. The quilt template used in the scrapbook page presented on the opposite page is a wonderful way to piece together a quilt pattern to set off the tender images of parents with their newborn infant. The quilt reminds us of tradition, of family; the photos speak solidly of warmth and love.

▶ *FLORAL QUILT, by Scarlett Clay, Leander, TX. This page, inspired by a magazine quilt pattern, is a clever and decorative way to use lots of pictures. To make a quilt pattern or template, photocopy and enlarge to the appropriate size the scrapbook page as shown on the facing page, or try drawing your own templates. Then use the templates to crop your photos. The flowers/leaf pieces, stems, and frames can be cut from patterned paper (as these were), or try painting some paper yourself before cutting it.*

Jacob's 1st Year

Cupid's Calendar

Each picture taken on the 14th of every month starting with February 14, 1995

The idea of photos in a context is of particular importance and probably most evident with baby pages. We observe the growth of a child in stages and compare these stages to other benchmarks—size, abilities, interests, etc. A year's worth of photos of Jacob (*shown opposite*) in the same chair with the same teddy bear on the same day of each month is a wonderful synthesis of growth in an infant's first year. "Cupid's Calendar"— Jacob was a Valentine's Day baby—is clever and perfectly appropriate.

Theme pages are a great way to use up extra or miscellaneous photos. Consider a "picture perfect" page that includes great photos not linked to other pages. A page that features your baby in different settings and times with a special toy is another possibility. Some scrapbookers use color to pull a layout together. Simply choose photos with a similar color scheme and use the color in the title for the page.

TIP: SAVE EVERYTHING!

Baby Memorabilia & Photo Checklist:
Shower invitations
Wrapping paper or ribbons
Photos of baby "equipment"
Ultrasound pictures
Bassinet name tag
Doctor's business card
Photo of hospital and nursery
Hospital and official birth certificates
Hospital bracelet
Handprints and footprints
Hospital bill
Birth announcement
Newspaper birth announcement
Cards from family and friends
Gift list and registry
Baby food, formula, and diaper labels
Growth and development records
Lock of hair
Small articles of clothing
Baby pictures of mom and dad

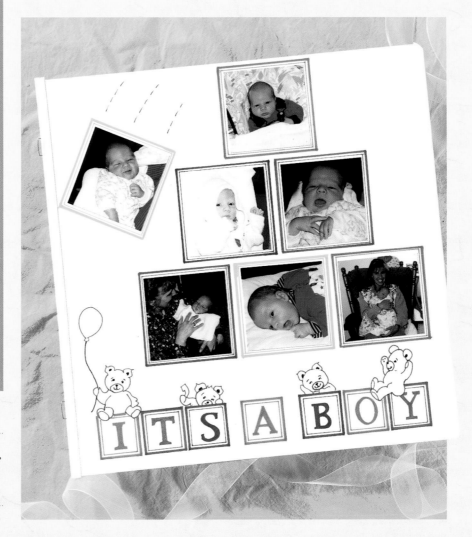

▶ *IT'S A BOY! by Karin Hrywko, Orlando, FL.*
A grandson's birth announcement functions as the design theme for the first page.

◀ *JACOB'S 1ST YEAR, by Renee Belina, Apple Valley, MN.*

▲ BABY SHOWER, *by Yuko Neal, Huntington Beach, CA. A baby shower for a sister provides the inspiration for these pretty pages. Using different border designs of the same color for each page—there are ten in all—simultaneously unifies and highlights the acitivities of the party.*

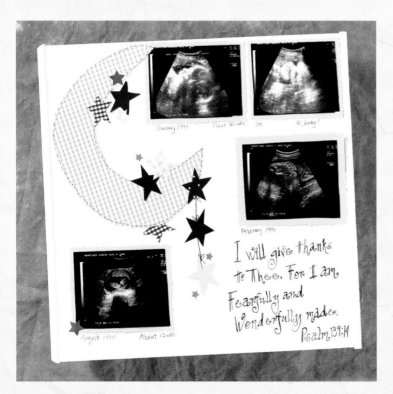

▲ IT'S JUST INTERMISSION, *by Kim Bunton, Bloomington, IN. We can all relate to Kim's story. All she wanted was an angelic picture of Samantha in the dress given to her by her grandparents. But what she ended up with was a picture of Samantha in a different mood, furious at her mother for having put her in such an uncomfortable dress! The mats for the photo and journaling labels reiterate a dominant color in the background printed paper and serve to bring our focus to the less-than-happy infant dressed in her finest.*

◀ I WILL GIVE THANKS SONOGRAM, *by Kimberly Moore, Hutchinson, KS. First photos of your baby need not be taken after the baby's birth. With today's technology, we can have a record of every step along the way, in pictures that could certainly be the first in your baby's book.*

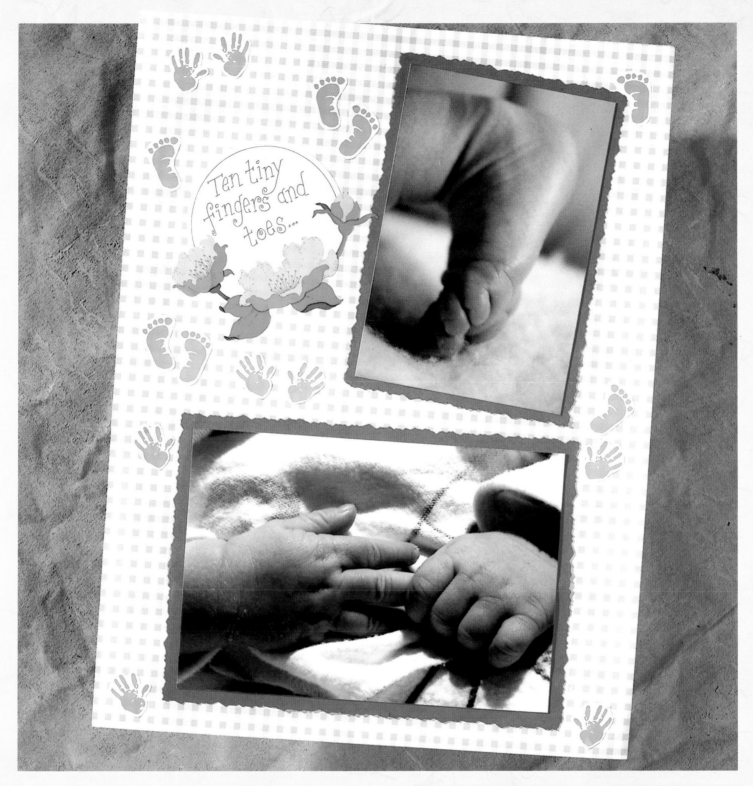

▲ TEN TINY FINGERS & TOES, *by Kristi Hazelrigg, Seminole, OK. Nothing typifies a new baby more than fingers and toes. How many times did we as new mothers count them? The simple black-and-white photos cradled in pink capture the dreamy mood.*

▶▶*(Overleaf)* CALEB'S BULLETIN BOARD, *by Kelly Clauss, Yorba Linda, CA. A charming bulletin board clearly reflects the goings-on in a typical home with active children. The informal placement of the photos and the decorative push pin art add a casual look to the page.*

to do list:

1. Kiss my mommy
2. play w/ daddy
3. sleep
4. eat
5. stroller ride
6.

MOMMY

▲ *VALENTINE HEART PAPER PIERCING, by Pam Klassen, Denver, CO. Photo by Eric Wilbur.*

PAPER PIERCING

Creative scrapbookers find inspiration almost anywhere. Paper piercing evolved from fifteenth-century parchment craft, which uses a number of techniques to create a design on parchment paper. Our basic example uses the techniques of embossing, cross-hatching, piercing, and perforating to yield an exquisite, lace-like design. To make the fancy heart frame, first photocopy and enlarge the heart design to the desired size. Use a dark pen to trace along the lines, making them easier to see. Then tape parchment paper over the pattern and trace with a white pencil or pen. Do not trace the cross-hatching. Now follow these steps:

STEP 1.

After tracing your design, place it right side down on an embossing pad, dense felt, or a computer mouse pad. Use an embossing tool (stylus) to trace along the white lines, applying enough pressure to change the parchment from gray to white. Fill in areas by gently rubbing the stylus from side to side, gradually increasing the pressure as the paper turns white.

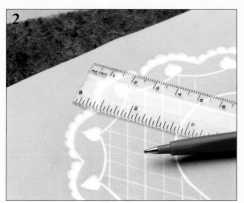

STEP 2.

To cross-hatch, place your design right side down on an embossing pad. Use a ruler and a fine-tipped embossing stylus to emboss the grid lines. Press lightly so that the cross-hatches appear fainter than your embossed lines.

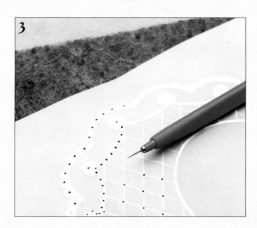

STEP 3.

To pierce, place your design on a thick felt pad. Using a piercing tool, pierce your design as desired. Pierce the parchment paper so that the colored paper you will eventually place under the parchment will show through the pierced spots. If you are piercing for decoration along a line, leave at least the width of one hole between each piercing.

STEP 4.

To remove an outside edge or inside section, pierce just outside the embossed edges, placing the holes very close together (basically creating a perforated edge, ready for smooth tearing). To tear away the waste paper, press down near the perforated line and gently remove the waste paper.

SUPPLIES

❖ *Parchment and colored papers*
❖ *Embossing pad and stylus*
❖ *Piercing tool*
❖ *White pencil or pen*

CREATING A PUZZLE PAGE

This page uses the Coluzzle®—a sturdy plastic template that lets you crop photos into perfectly inter-locking puzzle pieces. Coluzzles allow you to fit together several pictures into neat puzzle shapes, much like children's jigsaw puzzles. The templates are available in rectangle, star, heart, oval, teddy bear, and flowerpot shapes. These templates offer a completely new approach to cropping photos. This teddy bear Coluzzle (*shown opposite*) offers a whimsical way to combine five different photos in one 8 x 10-inch space. See Sources (page 116) for the Coluzzle Scrapbooking Kit. Each kit includes a reusable template, a swivel knife designed specifically for the Coluzzle template channels, a straight knife for trimming, and a foam cutting mat (a regular self-healing mat will not work with the swivel knife).

1. GATHER PHOTOS AND PLAN LAYOUT

Collect photos and determine which to use for each puzzle piece. Use the template to make sure each photo fits the corresponding piece. To keep the focus on the page, subjects should face forward or toward the center of the layout.

2. CROP THE PHOTOS

For each puzzle piece, orient the photo as desired under the template. Place the photo and template on top of a foam cutting mat. Securely holding the template over the photo, place the tip of the swivel knife within each cutting channel and cut along each edge of the template.

3. TRIM PIECES AND ASSEMBLE

Remove the template and use a straight knife or scissors to make the final trims that connect each cutting line. Carefully remove the finished puzzle piece from the photo background. Assemble and arrange the design on your scrapbook page. A repositionable adhesive will allow you to move the pieces around before permanently bonding the design to your page. Embellish and journal as desired.

▶ *A BEARY SPECIAL GIRL, by Gail Means, Escondido, CA, and Marie Lariviere, Hanover, MA.*

good things come in small boxes

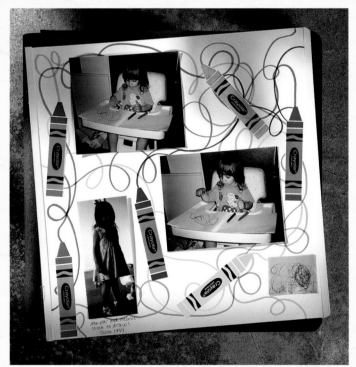

► QUINN'S 2ND BIRTHDAY, by Amy E. Carrell, Des Moines, IA. A giant freehand-cut numeral almost fills the page and certainly fills the bill. We know what to celebrate here. Silhouetted photos mounted strategically around the large "2" keep the birthday boy in focus. Decorative stickers embellish the colorful page.

◄ HANDLE WITH CARE, by Linda Rozolis, Cary, IL. Isn't it true? Kids have more fun with the packaging than what's in it! The large box was freehand cut and filled with matted photos.

▼ FIRST DRAWING, by Marsha Peacock, Jacksonville, FL. Here's the perfect time to let your children scribble right on the page. Thick colored pens and crayon stickers are all the supplies you need, in addition to the photos and a little art direction.

◄ 15 MONTHS OLD, by Ellen Underhill, Seattle, WA. A simple tic-tac-toe design turns this record of Aiden's first fifteen months into a pleasingly organized page of simple shapes alive with bright colors and easy-to-read journaling.

happy birthday 2 you! September 9, 1997

Daddy helps Quinn learn how to blow out the candles. Daddy has had a lot of practice!!

Quinn is getting the hang of opening presents!

your 2nd birthday was low key. We celebrated with a small party. Our guests were Judy, Jim and Jack, Karen and Luanne and Grandma Garrett. We had dinner, ice cream, cake, balloons and presents!

Good job, Quinn, you did it!

Quinn, I didn't take too long! What a lot to get!!

Quinn, modeling his new Elmo back pack from the Quick-Spanian family.

Luanne told Quinn to "up" when she took this picture. Who Look at these cheeks!

happy birthday 2

happy birthday 2 you! happy birthday 2 you! happy birthday 2 you!

happy birthday 2 you!

"Q" turns

September 10, 1997

Quinn Turns 2 years old in Des Moines, Iowa

Toys! GLORIOUS TOYS!

Look at all these presents - I can handle this!

YiPeeeeeee!!!

Quinn in his jammies the morning of his birthday. He is playing with all of his new toys from his party the night before. He got a lot of trucks and emergency vehicles.

HAPPY BIRTHDAY

2

Here is Quinn on September 12, 1997. This is his very first day of school at Bankford Children's Center. He could not start until after his 2nd birthday. My little boy is growing up!

Up bright to early, child feeling a bit tired! What a week!

2

CHILDREN

Kids do the darnedest things! Before you know it, your child will be a teen, and those innocent days of discovery will be past. Don't miss the opportunity to record those precious years. Children's activities offer so many themes to choose from. Children play. They learn. Go off to school. Lose their baby teeth. Learn to ride a bicycle and skip rope. Learn to read and write. Develop friendships. Test boundaries. And all of it is done with individual style and filled with unique moments.

The possibilities for preserving these memories are as varied as the memories themselves. And these memory books help develop your child's self-esteem. They help children know who they are at an early age and instill a sense of security and worth. Why not create a storybook in which your child is the main character in a cast of family, friends, and pets? You may either write your own story or adapt a favorite one, substituting your child for the central character. Create a song book using pictures of your child to illustrate the words. Including early artwork will further personalize an album of your child's formative years, and delight her in the process.

This chapter features an interesting way to present children's portraits. Pages 38 and 39 outline a really neat technique that will give a 3-D effect to your pages, making your children's portraits seem to pop off the page. However you decide to save the history, you and your child will enjoy looking back to today.

▶ *CARYN LOVES HER ALFAFANATOR, by Joyce Feil, Littleton, CO. Caryn's affection for her horse and the relationship they have is extraordinary. The larger photograph allows us to see their mutual affection. The horse could not possibly wrap his neck around her any more* *than he has already. And no one will come between the two of them. The classically simple presentation allows the photos to speak for themselves. The arches make us feel as though we are looking into a barn stall at an everyday activity.*

KC

CARYN LOVES HER ALFAFANATOR

CREATE A PICTURE BOOK

Children love picture books. Little ones enjoy learning new words, talking about the pictures, or even making up stories of their own. Why not make a picture book with and about your child? An animal picture book is perfect for photos you've taken of your child at the zoo. Your child will learn animal names, and you'll both have fun creating the pages!

◀ TREE CLIMBERS, by Sandra Blair, Canyon Country, CA. What could be more natural than kids climbing trees on a bright spring day? The photos themselves become an extension of the trees they are in. Sandra has echoed the palette of the leafy branches in her bold artwork. Her trees look as natural as the real ones! And this she accomplishes using colored paper, stamps, and a sponge to add texture. Freehand touches provide additional texture to the tree trunks. Flower and insect stickers finish the page.

▲ APPLE SCHOOL DAYS, by Carrie Davis, Everett, WA. Children peering out from red, green, and golden apples bring smiles of remembrance of school days for all of us. This first-grade teacher more than met the annual challenge of how to incorporate individual school pictures into her scrapbook. The "apple" theme allowed her to include lots of photos in a small space. Photos were cropped with a circle template. The jaunty freehand-cut apples in a carefree arrangement give formal school portraits a new look.

PRESERVING CHILDREN'S ARTWORK

If your child's drawing or painting is too large to include in your album, have a color photocopy made, reducing the image to fit the page. Silhouette cropping of the artwork emphasizes the handmade quality. Or you may want to include a photo of the actual item that was drawn or painted, as well as a photo of the young artist.

If you have a particularly prolific budding artist in your ranks, take a weekly or monthly photo of the child with the accomplishments of that period. This will give you a record of the growing child as well as the talent!

TIP: PHOTO OP

Carry your camera with you to take advantage of opportunities to capture images that might suggest a theme for your scrapbook pages.

Best Buds...

Allison and Josh

Playing with their sidewalk

Fall, 1997

3-D ELEMENTS

Bring depth to your pages with this 3-D technique. The process is simple and adds immeasurable interest. Select an area of a photo you want to emphasize. With this process a figure or group of figures, a flower—or anything you want—can be literally brought forward. It's really best to lay out your whole page before deciding which elements to emphasize. You might choose elements from various spots in the photo. And to create a balanced composition, you should see the whole scene ahead of time.

STEP 1.
Gather two copies of each photo that you want to make three-dimensional. Cut out the element you want to emphasize with the 3-D effect.

STEP 2.
Adhere generous amounts of double-sided padded adhesive to the backs of the silhouetted portions. Position the silhouetted portions on the uncut photograph in the same positions.

◄ *Best Buds, by Theresa McFayden, Omaha, NE.*

PUNCHES

Punch art adds even more dimension to this 3-D photo page. Punch art is easy to do, and with the large number of available punches and the many different papers available, the possibilities are astronomical! See Sources on page 116 for other images and information. You'll find punch art used on several pages throughout this book. For more instruction see pages 63 and 73. This project uses the following punches:

❖ *For Large Flowers—large circle, snipped for yellow flower*
❖ *For Large Flower Centers—small circle*
❖ *For Small Flowers—small circle*
❖ *For Small Flower Centers—1/4-inch round punch*
❖ *For Flower Leaves—birch leaf and small circle cut in half*
❖ *For Heart Accents—small and mini hearts*

▶▶ *(Overleaf)* HUGS AND KISSES TO THE SCARECROW, *by Donna Leicht, Appleton, WI. Lazy summer days on the farm. Hugs and kisses and more hugs and kisses as brother and sister take their turn greeting a treasured scarecrow. Each look at these cheery pages, with pictures of their favorite activities on the farm framed by summer-bright colored papers and even different colored checked borders, will bring happy memories of days in Door Country, Wisconsin, flooding back. The disarming photos are set off with bright colored mats.*

Hugs and Kisses to
The Farm's
Scarecrow!

Sarah loved this
Lassie-like collie named
Laddie. Laddie loved
herding so much that
she herded the baby
chicks back into the
chicken hut! This black
Pygmy goat was Sarah's
favorite. She held him
the entire week.

The currents are a little sour,
but yummy!

More Hugs and Kisses to The
Farm's Scarecrow!

Was this really how kids got water to
drink in the olden days? It's fun!

LETTERING STYLES

Sometimes it's fun to experiment with different lettering styles. The bold lowercased alphabet (complete with a few backward letters) shown here is reminiscent of those used to teach the ABCs and is perfect for your children's scrapbook pages. Trace and use these or experiment with your own. The decorative alphabet included below can be copied by machine, or try copying this style freehand.

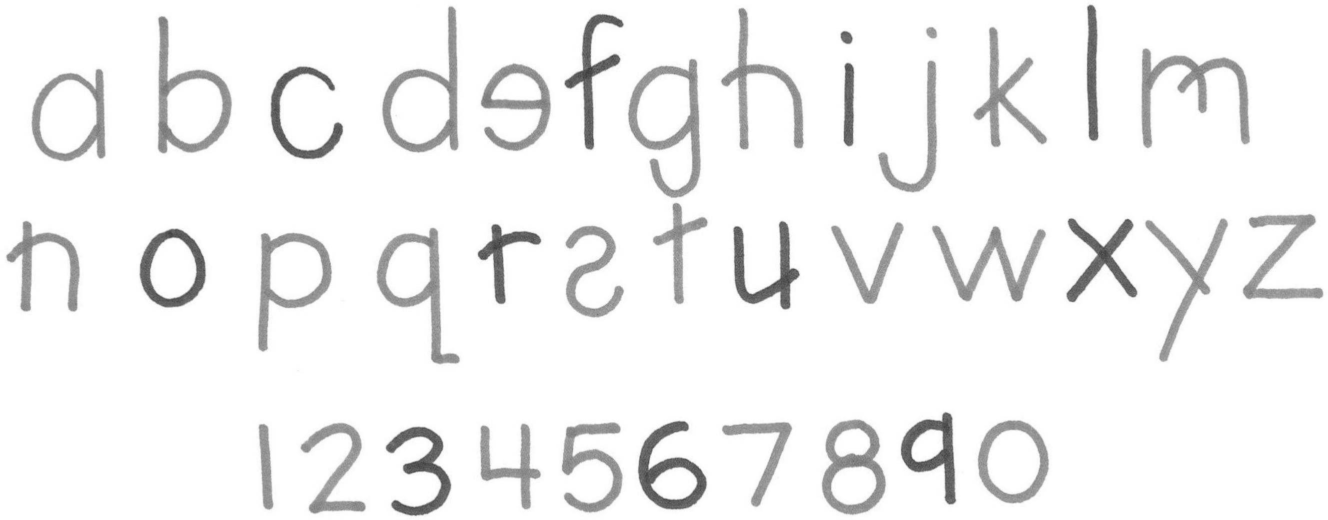

abcdefghijklm
nopqrstuvwxyz
1234567890

Letterstyle by Jennifer Johnston.

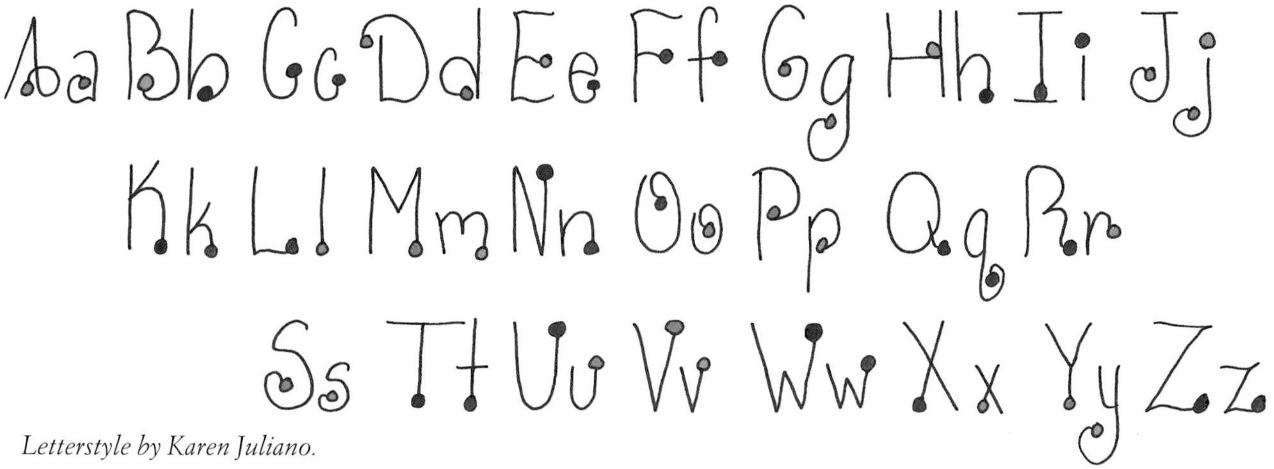

Aa Bb Cc Dd Ee Ff Gg Hh Ii Jj
Kk Ll Mm Nn Oo Pp Qq Rr
Ss Tt Uu Vv Ww Xx Yy Zz

Letterstyle by Karen Juliano.

▶ROUGH & TUMBLE, *by Pam Klassen, Denver, CO. Photos by Alison Beachem. The playground is a natural place to take action shots of your children and their friends. The "kids" lettering style, applied with different colored pens, accentuates the youthfulness of this page.*

PETS

Whether small, large, furry, feathered, or scaly, pets enrich our lives and never fail to entertain. Their curious ways often volunteer them as the subject on the other side of a camera, and they always seem to outdo themselves with a new snapshot-worthy antic. Through their interesting personalities and achievements, or simply by virtue of their birth, pets hold an important place in family life. And for scrapbookers, that means a prominent place in the family photo album.

Photographing pets poses an interesting challenge—we've yet to find a dog who will obey the commands, "Sit, look pretty, and smile. Hold that." To help with that problem, we've included some tips for taking pet portraits on page 48. We've also included a how-to section on photo kaleidoscopes, an exciting technique that produces almost awe-inspiring results. Although the end products may look complex, don't be afraid to try.

The first "hello" from your feathered friend, your kitten's roll with a ball of yarn, your dog's graduation from obedience school—pet milestones are perfect fare for a scrapbook. If you have one or two pets, consider compiling pet-style baby books which record birth, significant firsts, and loving family members. If you have a large pet family, try making one spread for each member. Include the best pictures, write down factual information, journal about a funny memory. Your scrapbook can be one of the best ways to record for all just what your pets mean to you.

▶ *MORGAN ST. CROIX, by Sandra de St. Croix, St. Albert, Alberta, Canada. Some golden retrievers do know how to sit and pose regally for a portrait. Morgan St. Croix is one of them, and here he poses amid a mosaic-like pattern of tulip photos in his garden, basking in nature's bounty. The bright yellow and green freehand-cut letters spelling out his name tumble across the tulips. The garden photos are cropped in simple rectangular shapes creating a soft blanket of color around the master.*

CREATING PHOTO KALEIDOSCOPES™

Photo kaleidoscopes are "hands-on" art at its finest. Kaleidoscopes are intriguing and may seem complicated, but they are quick and simple to make using an equal number of regular and reversed photos.

▲ *SOPHIE JEWELL, page by Pam Klassen, Denver, CO.; kaleidoscope by Kathleen Paneitz, Longmont, CO. What better way to show off a furry friend than featuring her not once, but eight times! The effect is sophisticated, but the process is simpler than it looks.*

SELECT THE PHOTO

The most dramatic kaleidoscope effects are produced with photos that have repetitive patterns, intersecting lines, vivid colors, good light quality, and lots of activity.

DETERMINE CUTTING LINES

Place a clear plastic triangle (we've found that a 45-degree triangle is the easiest to work with) over the part of the photo you want to use. Place the edges on a part of the photo that will make an interesting pattern when matched with a reversed image. Holding a mirror against the side of the triangle can help you visualize this.

1. The original Sophie Jewell portrait.

DETERMINE NUMBER OF REPRINTS

Imagine the part of the photo you've chosen to use as a slice of pie. The angle you use will determine the number of slices needed; the angles must add up to 360 degrees, the number of degrees that make a circle.

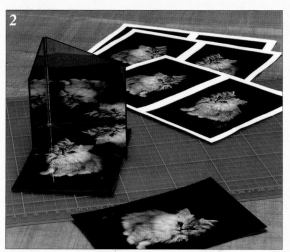

ORDER REPRINTS

Have the photo lab make reprints of your original photo and the reversed image. If you decided to use a 45-degree angle, you'll need eight photos—four originals and four reversed images (a 60-degree angle needs 6 photos—3 originals and 3 reversed; a 30-degree angle needs 12 photos—6 originals and 6 reversed).

2. Eight copies of the original photo—four regular and four reversed. (Ask a photo shop to provide prints from your negatives.)

CUT PHOTOS

Lay the triangle over the part of the photo you want to use. Find at least three reference points that fall along the edge of the triangle and cut through these exact points on each original and reversed image photo.

ASSEMBLE CUT PIECES

Place one cut piece of an original beside one cut piece of a reversed image, matching along your reference points. Repeat with all pairs and assemble the pairs into a star.

ADD FINISHING TOUCHES

Trim the outside edge in a pleasing pattern. Mount the kaleidoscope on a scrapbook page using double-sided tape. Embellish the page as desired.

3. Using a 45-degree angle, crop the photos to create a pleasing pattern. Arrange in the shape of a star.

▶ BASKET OF PUPPIES, *by Nina Hershberger, Elkhart, IN.*

▶▶ EMBER AT PISMO BEACH, *by Jennifer Jae Barber, San Jose, CA.*

▼ DAISY, *photograph by Jim Cambon, Fort Collins, CO.*

TAKING BETTER PET PORTRAITS

As with babies, photographing pets poses certain challenges because you can't just tell them to sit and smile for the camera. But with a little know-how, you'll get good results.

❖ *Select the right film. Choose fast film such as ISO 400 or 800 for clear action shots; use ISO 100 or 200 for stills.*
❖ *Choose a setting that accentuates your pet's personality and physical traits. For example, if your cat is a great lounger, you might photograph her in an easy chair, or stretched across a windowsill waiting for an unfortunate bird or mouse to venture forth.*
❖ *Clean and groom your pet before a sitting, possibly removing collars and tags.*
❖ *Take lots of photographs whenever you can. Your pet just might get used to it, and you'll have a better chance of getting some interesting shots.*
❖ *Don't be afraid of bribery. Small animal treats work wonders. Most professional animals are trained this way.*
❖ *You can control your pet's behavior. If you're quiet, chances are your pet will respond in a similar fashion.*

MBER

Pismo Beach
August 8, 1998

TEENS

You've come a long way, baby. Your "child" is now driving a car, earning a paycheck from an after-school job, soaring as an athlete, getting ready for the prom, thinking about and maybe even planning for the future. Perfect fodder for new scrapbook pages! Teen albums capture the years of constant change. They can also help teens recognize their strengths—perhaps even revealing future talents. Here are a few ideas for commemorating your child's teenage years.

A life album may summarize years one to eighteen and include birth, school days, and graduation. It could also include other important events such as a school play, a trip, an adventure with a special friend or grandparents, or a camping trip. You might also focus a teen album on one major activity such as sports, music, or theater. Activity albums allow you to focus on the details—documenting the span of a varsity football career could fill a hundred pages. A third option is to create a personal yearbook with social and academic highlights. A personal yearbook can tell the story of those memorable high school years from your teen's unique point of view. Page subjects might include passing her driver's test, the first date, induction into the honor society, a concert or recital, graduation, and awards.

There are as many techniques for producing your pages as there are possible themes. In this section we've included instructions for layered roses, just the thing for accenting a prom page, or commemorating any special event.

▶ PINK DIAMOND SOCCER, by Claudia Hill, Whittier, CA. Creating a page devoted to your teen's favorite pastime, whether it be sports or another activity, goes a long way to building self-esteem. With sports, team colors are the way to go, and in this case what great colors those are! Take advantage of the available die cuts, stickers, and printed papers to make a unique and personalized page that says it all.

AYSO 1993

▼ *GOLF LESSON, by Jeanne Ciolli, Lake Forest, CA. Whether over, under, or right at par, most golfers take their time on the links very seriously. They look for improvement every time out, and they often find it. Photograph your teen striving for that perfect game. If you're lucky, you'll capture better and better strokes with each outing. This page was assembled with a scorecard, stickers, colored papers, and golf balls cut from a magazine.*

TEEN THEMES AND MEMORABILIA

Learning to drive, learner's permit, first car, copy of driver's license
Learning to change a tire
Locker decorations
Favorite teachers, coaches, mentors, and lessons learned from them
Special friends and family members
After-school jobs, first paycheck
Favorite clothes, fads, and munchies
Favorite places and hangouts
Applying for college, SATs, campus visits, top college picks
First date, dances, and proms
Current events and political interests
Bedroom decor
Weekend sleep schedule
Activities and achievements
Popular music, movies, and television programs
Changing hairstyles, first shave
Blank pages for friends to sign

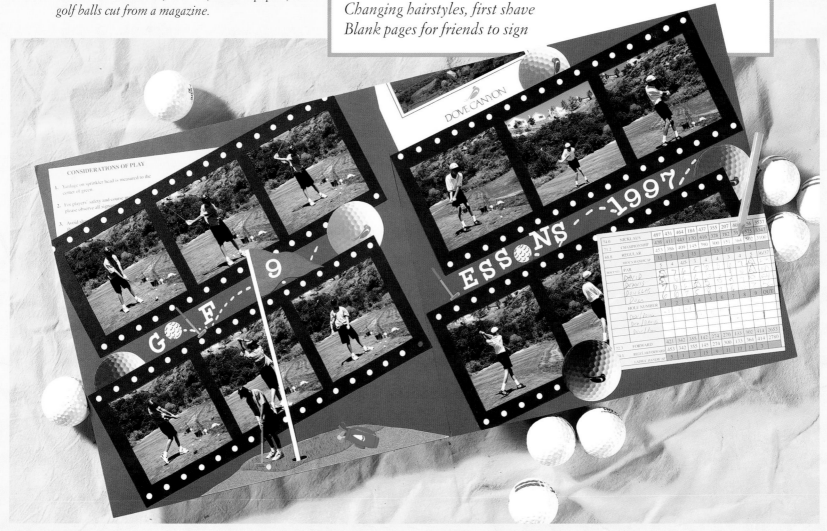

◀ *SKATEBOARD RAMP, by Dianne Gottron, Hollister, CA. Playing with proportions and placement, Dianne has emphasized how high her son was skating—leaping tall buildings, soaring over treetops. Action shots such as these are favorites among teens and their parents alike. When looking at them in your scrapbook, you can almost hear the shouts of, "Look, Ma. No hands!" The houses, fence, and trees are freehand cut, and the ridges on the house and fence were created with an embossing stylus and ridged stencil.*

◀ *BAND DAY, by Jennifer Weeks, Tempe, AZ. Here's a wonderful example of how much a very simple page can express. These pages are some of Jennifer's first efforts, and we think they're very effective. When she cut the musical note from the blue background, she didn't want to just toss it, so she incorporated it into the design of the facing page. The note is freehand cut, and photos are cropped to complement that shape.*

▲ WHERE'S EVAN? *by Diane Stanley, Yorba Linda, CA. High school graduation is one of those exciting once-in-a-lifetime events that you will definitely want to capture on film. But it's easy to get carried away and find yourself with too many photographs that look a bit too similar. That's what happened here, and a page based on the* Where's Waldo *books is both humorous and practical. Extra photos are cut into triangles and arranged maze-like as borders around the page.*

▶ RYAN'S FIRST CAR, *by Carolyn Kissel, Bradenton, FL. Carolyn Kissel created a whole line of printed news items called "Seems Like Yesterday" to add historical journaling to her scrapbook pages. If you want to place your photos in an earlier time and place, try one of her products. (See Sources on page 116.) If your photos are current, use newspaper and magazine clippings to tell the story.*

A HAPPY GRAD

I'M WEARING A WHITE ROSE CORSAGE. LOOKING BEAUTIFUL!

I'M WEARING A BEADED BAG.... A GLORIOUS ANTIQUE.

CAITLYNN, HWIE LIE AND HER MOM - PROUD MOM

YOU GUYS LOOK GREAT!

CHARLIE   VINCE   JEFF
GRAD '98

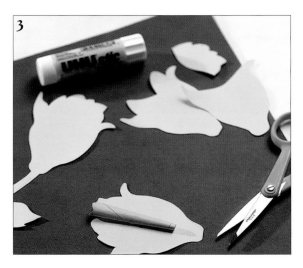

Creating a Layered Rose

This elegant three-dimensional flower was made using a commercially available flower die cut. (See Sources on page 116.) For one flower, you need eight identical rose die cuts—seven in the color of the petals and one in green for the stem. To add shading to the rose, purchase petal die cuts in two shades of the same color. Shape "a" shows what each die cut looks like at the outset. You will be cutting as shown to create the individual shapes to form the layered rose. All letters "a" through "h" in these instructions refer to the lettered images shown here, top left.

1. Create the Base

To create the base of the rose, trim die cuts "a" and "b" as illustrated, cutting away the portions shown in black. Roll die cut "b" cigar style and adhere to the middle of die cut "a." Set aside to dry.

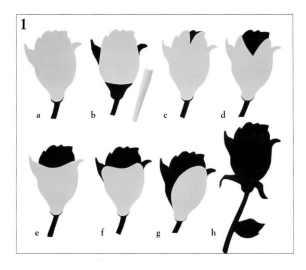

2. Trim Die Cuts

Trim and adhere petals "c" through "g," cutting away the portions in black. Fold forward the tips of each petal, or use a round item such as a pen barrel to roll the tips forward. Layer and adhere the petals one on top of another on the base in order "c" through "g." Rounded petals will flatten out a little when stored in a scrapbook.

3. Adhere the Stem

To create the stem, trim die cut "h" as shown. Adhere the stem on top of the rose base. To add dimension to the stem, trim leaves from an extra green die cut and adhere them to your stem base. To add dimension to the stem and leaf, use an additional green die cut.

◄ *Pretty in Pink and Silver and Prom Guys, by Linda Schell, North Vancouver, British Columbia, Canada. Roses are a special symbol in the life of Linda's daughter Cait. So Linda constructed roses in paper to embellish commemorative pages. The Pretty in Pink and Silver page uses rose-printed paper to echo the theme. The photos are triple-mounted with mats cut with fancy scissors, and silver rose stickers add the final touch. For Prom Guys, Linda freehand cut a "tuxedo" shape from printed and black and white papers. The red rose in the lapel is a dapper detail.*

HERITAGE

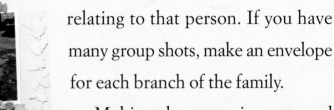

There is no better gift you can give your family than their heritage, beautifully and accurately recorded for future generations. One of the most important elements of creating your heritage album is research. Read everything available about your family, and talk with older relatives about their memories. Each person will have a different perspective of the same event, so don't be surprised if you hear many versions of the same story! Use the information you collect for journaling—it will bring the pictures to life.

The other major element to gather for your album is photographs, and keeping them organized is vital. Consider starting an envelope for each member of the family to keep together all photos, documents, stories, and mementos relating to that person. If you have many group shots, make an envelope for each branch of the family.

Making the pages is next, and there is no right or wrong way to design your heritage album. Ask yourself a few simple questions. How much time and money do I want to invest? Are most of my photos from one era or do I have a mix of time periods? Do I want a simple or ornate design? The answers to these questions will help determine the direction of your design.

The technique of paper punch art on page 63 may be used to create many different styles of pages that can convey a specific time and place. We've seen many beautiful heritage pages over the years, and present only a few of our favorites here.

▶ *THE ROARING 20s, by Cheryl Thomas, Crackerjack Too, Highland, CA. Heirloom photos and stories hold a special place in the hearts of many of us, and making scrapbook pages with them is a special treat. The content, texture, and general feeling of this page bring the roar-ing 20s to life. The background paper used here is preprinted, but you could also make your own with genuine keepsake letters and a photo-copy machine. The deep, rich, jewel-toned colors on this page add a sumptuous dimension and sophistication.*

The "ROARING" 20's

FREEDOM!

FUN!

DICKEY—BOY" and MAY!

FLAPPERS!

FORD!

TOP ROW: JANE DOYLE, MARY JANE JONES,
MARY NIEDRINGHAUS, LOUISE GILMORE, &
MARY HELEN RIESTEAD.
BOTTOM ROW: EVELYN PLACK, CAROLINE COX, & ME!

CAT

◄ HOW DID WE MEET? *by Joyce Schweitzer, Greensboro, NC. Joyce is creating a scrapbook for her parents, and she mails them a new section of the book every few weeks as it is completed. Imagine the anticipation with which each package is opened! When her parents look back at the pictures and mementos, they recognize the glamour and the love in their marriage all over again. The simple techniques of paper cutting and matting used here evoke a very specific mood.*

► THE WHITAKER CHILDREN, *by Cheryl Thomas, Crackerjack Too, Highland, CA. Here is another use of the popular quilt theme for a page of old family photos. Designed to represent the simplicity of the old midwest, this page does just that. Shapes are punched from the yellow die cuts and four of the removed sections are used as corner decorations on the photograph. Drawn stitches and real buttons are delightful finishing details.*

►► FAMILY TREE, *by Allison Garman, Jefferson, MD. Here's the result of blending two passions—genealogy and scrapbooking. Allison is fortunate enough to have photographs of ancestors as far back as six great-great grandparents. She even added a few branches for those grandparents for whom she did not have photos. Start your tree with a picture of yourself, and build back in time. An allover pattern of stamped leaves creates the background used here and the tree branches are drawn with a watercolor pen.*

margaret and Patti 1947 Marietta, Ga.

◄ VICTORIAN PICTURE FRAME, by Marilyn Garner, San Diego, CA. This pretty assemblage of punch art has a bit of a Victorian flavor and is a great way to accent heirloom photographs. These flowers make use of fifteen different punches, and the result is both dressy and delicate. There is no limit to what you can do with punch art. Here the original punched shapes are hardly recognizable—the pieces are folded and combined with others to create uniquely styled flowers.

PUNCH ART FRAME

The simplicity of punch art has made it one of the most popular ways we know to create captivating pages. All you need are a few punches and some paper to make unique art for your scrapbook pages. Our paper artists marvel at how rapidly punch art projects take on a life of their own, adding charm and whimsy to scrapbook pages, photo frames, cards, invitations, and more. With a little imagination and a few punches, you can construct fabulous pages with extraordinary depth and dimension. Follow the steps below to construct the exquisite picture frame seen opposite.

STEP 1.

A small flower bud is constructed by snipping a small egg with a mini sun and layering it over another small egg, then layering it on top with a medium tulip.

STEP 2.

Portions of a small snowflake are layered over a small bell, then layered with a medium tulip to make a bell flower.

STEP 3.

A large flower bud is created by layering three small strawberries over a small egg.

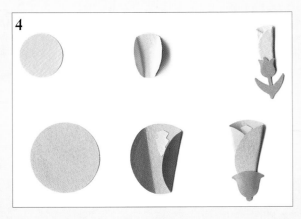

STEP 4.

To create tubular flowers, fold circles in thirds and layer with a tulip or bell and a portion of the snowflake.

TIP: KEEPING PUNCHES SHARP

When punches become dull, try punching through aluminum foil to sharpen. Or, to sharpen all edges, punch through a very fine grade of sandpaper in both directions (upside-down and right-side up).

Mosaic Beach Scene, by Denise Tucker, Versailles, IN. Photos from a beach vacation are cut and repieced into various sea-related shapes.

SPECIAL

EVENTS

WEDDINGS

While your wedding may be a one-day, once-in-a-lifetime event, the opportunities for celebrating the occasion in your scrapbook are countless. Whether you're a bride-to-be or have celebrated milestone anniversaries, any time is a good time to plan or rethink your wedding album. Many of us spend vast amounts of time, energy, and money to make our wedding day a day unlike any other. And like everything related to this most special day, you want your wedding scrapbook to be exquisite, beautiful, breathtaking—in short, perfect.

There are as many different ways to style a wedding album as there are styles of weddings. If your wedding was simple and elegant, you may want your commemorative book to reflect that mood. If your wedding was colorful and gay, use bold pens and stickers to accentuate that tone. If your wedding took place years ago, consider creating an anniversary album that incorporates the theme or feeling of your wedding through the years since that day.

The pages shown opposite use simple, elegant frames to capture and preserve various moments of a wedding day. The scrapbook page featured on page 72 incorporates the technique of paper punch art to create a romantic setting for an heirloom wedding portrait. Punch art offers limitless options for creative expression. Literally hundreds of punches are available, and when you team them with boundless paper choices, you can create a page that is as unique as your experience. A book that captures the wonder of your wedding day will be treasured by you and your family for the life of the marriage and beyond.

▶ *WEDDING PORTRAITS, by Bev Klassen, Rosedale, British Columbia, Canada. These pages use simple, elegant frames to preserve memories of a daughter's wedding. The white frame featured on top is made from an embossed wedding invitation. You can create the right cropping for photos by matting with simple shapes. Freehand cut or use die cuts or punches to make flowers, buds, and leaves for the garland.*

Christine Suzanne Klassen and David Trenton Harms
April 12, 1997.

Among the greatest
of the gifts God sends—
Are those special people
We can call our Friends.

▲ KEITH AND SARA, by LeNae Gerig, Hot Off The Press, Canby, OR. With printed papers and ribbon, this page captures all the softness and romance of the bride's attire. A printed paper was laid down for the background, and scalloped strips cut following the design of the lacy paper are used for borders top and bottom. A satin ribbon bow adds just a touch of dimension, and a matted card with journaling records the date.

◄ WEDDING CAKE, by Eileen Ruscetta, Westminster, CO. Very often, wedding guests come with their cameras and will send you their favorite snapshots of the party. When you add them to the thousands your photographer took, you may be overwhelmed. Here's a clever way to use all those extra photos—cut them up and create a mosaic border. This border is pieced together with dozens of 1/2-inch squares, and the effect mimics the lattice-work background of the featured photographs.

▲ THE CAKE, *by Shelley Potter, Fairbanks, AK. Simple cropping and embellishing can speak volumes. The flower-covered arch at Shelly's reception inspired the shapes and design of this two-page spread of traditional cake-cutting activities. The border used here is preprinted, but you could also try drawing your own based on your photographs. A combination of many small stickers could also provide just the right touch. And don't forget the wonderful effects that can be created with fancy scissors.*

◄ WEDDING DANCERS, *by Kathleen Phelan, Baltimore, MD. If you're lucky, you may get a fabulous candid photograph from your wedding party like this one taken by photojournalist Perry Thorsvick. This shot is full of love and celebration, and is enhanced by simple embellishments. The ribbon border is created with colored pens and a wavy ruler. Simply draw one line, then move the ruler a bit to the right and draw another line. Connect the ends and color in.*

TIP: CROP IT RIGHT

When photographing people for your scrapbook page, get in close and keep your design simple.

Pictures at the
Ritz Carlton

Our photographer was Trish from Skinner-Vaughn Photography. As a special offer, she took us downtown two days before the wedding for some special pictures. These photos were taken at the Ritz Carlton Hotel on the Plaza. We also had pictures taken at the Nelson Atkins Art Gallery. Everyone we met treated us like king and queen.

▲ RITZ CARLTON, *by Ann Perry, Allen, TX. Friends and family members who weren't able to attend Ann's wedding say that looking through her album makes them feel as if they were there. Simple die cuts like the dove and heart used here convey a message of love and peace. Adding lots of journaling throughout the album will also help to tell the story of the day in its entirety, allowing loved ones to more fully realize the event. The decorative-edged frames for the photos add a romantic touch.*

▶ ▶ *(Overleaf)* WHITE-ON-WHITE WEDDING PAGE, *by Pam Klassen, Denver, CO. The beautiful punch art on this page creates a truly romantic setting for an heirloom wedding portrait. Creating the right ambiance for your photos goes a long way to telling their stories. And while this treatment may look complicated, it's done with only three punches. The instructions presented on page 73 tell you all you need to know to create punch art backgrounds that will be perfect for your scrapbook pages.*

Kane & Edna Ediger on their
Wedding Day October 4th 1936

PUNCH ART

Punch art can extend your scrapbooking budget by making good use of paper scraps that might otherwise be thrown away. With this project, punched art is used as delicate detailing providing a romantic soft white background on which the elegant historical photograph is presented. To make the delicate white-on-white background shown opposite, you need only three punches: a large circle, a small fleur-de-lis, and a diamond extension.

FLOWERS

Here we've combined two punched shapes to create a third. For each flower:

Step 1. Punch one shape using the diamond extension punch.

Step 2. Punch six fleur-de-lis shapes.

Step 3. Position the six fleur-de-lis shapes in a circle around a diamond and the flower is complete.

SWIRLS

We created crescents using a simple technique which we call offset punching. For each swirl:

Step 1. Punch one large circle from a sheet of paper.

Step 2. Flip the punch upside down and offset previously punched circle to create a crescent-shaped piece.

Step 3. Continue cutting crescents from the edge of the primary circle.

Step 4. Position the crescents on the page in alternating directions.

▼ *FLEUR-DE-LIS BORDER, by Debbie Hutchings, Longmont, CO. For this border we've combined multiples of the same shape to create a new one. Simply arrange four small fleur-de-lis shapes in a circle to create a flower. Connect the flowers to make a border.*

TRAVEL

No two things go more hand-in-hand than travel and picture taking. For many people, foreign travel is a once-in-a-lifetime opportunity that yields a much different vacation than hitting the local beach or visiting with family. That's not to say we have to go abroad to find memories that we'll treasure—your dream vacation may be in the next state, or even the next town. Wherever your travels may take you, there is no better way to preserve and later remember the splendor of the architecture, experiences, and people away from home than in a scrapbook.

The scrapbook page shown opposite uses simple borders created with paper and punches to mimic the architecture found in the American Southwest. Cutting and layering paper is a great way to create a page that represents the climate, terrain, and "feel" of your vacation spot. Take a good look at the interesting paper-layering technique presented on pages 84 and 85—it's almost as good as being there.

In addition to landmarks, take pictures of more ordinary sights—details of carvings in a church, a colorful garden, or even a local fruit-market vendor will add visual impact to your scrapbook. Collect memorabilia such as postcards, brochures, ticket stubs, postage stamps, currency, newspapers, and maps. Keeping a detailed journal of your travels will help you identify the sites you've photographed and add details the camera can't capture. Armed with your photos, memorabilia, and travel journal, you can relive the journey while creating your memory album.

▶ *CANYON ROAD INDIAN MARKET, by Debbie Hutchings, Longmont, CO. This page has the look and feel, almost the temperature, of the Southwest. Using only two punches, Debbie created borders that reflect the architecture in her photographs. For the top border, the top part of a small cross is punched into opposite sides of a paper strip. The same punch is used at an angle to create mats for lettering, and the page is finally embellished with the leftover bits from a southwest border punch.*

Canyon
Road
Indian
Market

Santa Fe
New Mexico

▲ CANYON LANDS NATIONAL PARK, *by Wendie Waldman, Silver City, NM. The vista in this national park is breathtaking, and well captured in these stunning photographs. Because the photographs are so open and inviting, keeping the pages that hold them fairly simple makes them seem even more vast. The muted color of the background paper provides an ideal base for these stunning images. Using embossing powder and rubber stamps, you can create textured images that will complement all kinds of photographs and styles of scrapbook pages.*

76

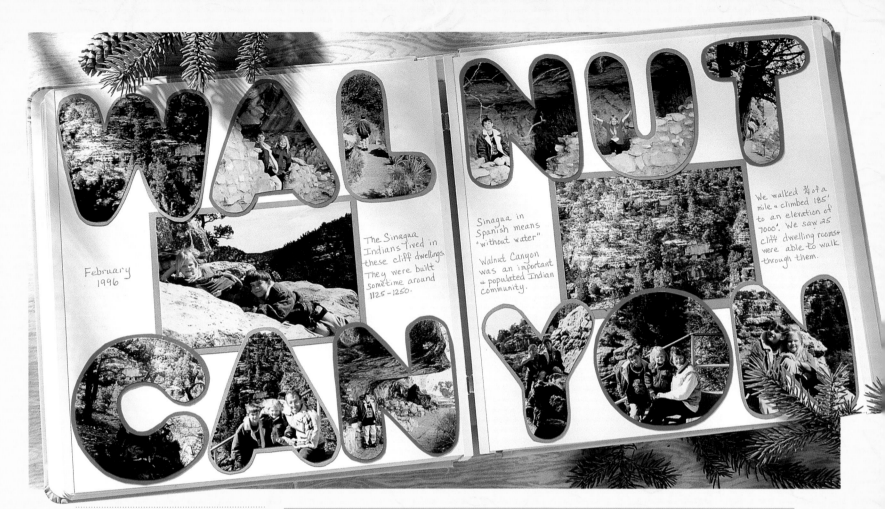

In the scrapbook photo letters spelling "WALNUT CANYON" with handwritten notes:

February 1996

The Sinagua Indians lived in these cliff dwellings. They were built sometime around 1125 - 1250.

Sinagua in Spanish means "without water"

Walnut Canyon was an important & populated Indian community.

We walked ¾ of a mile & climbed 185' to an elevation of 7000'. We saw 25 cliff dwelling rooms & were able to walk through them.

▲ WALNUT CANYON, *by Debbie Schubert, Phoenix, AZ. Photo letters is a technique that we love because it is so versatile. You can use it to create everything from fun and funky scrapbook pages to quiet and elegant ones. You may use purchased letter stencils or freehand your own unique alphabet. The technique is especially useful if you have many photographs from the same place. It's also an opportunity to use any less-than-perfect photographs that your children may have taken. A simple trim will turn them into works of art.*

TIPS FOR LETTERING TECHNIQUES

❖ *Practice makes perfect! If you are writing the letters freehand, you need to practice so you can feel the arc of the letters in your hand. If you are freehand cutting the letters out of cardstock or photos, practice with blank paper first.*

❖ *Keep the size of your page in mind when selecting letter style and size. Choose letters that will fit the space size and shape.*

❖ *When selecting a lettering style, always choose one that fits the tone of your page. Each style has its own personality.*

❖ *Experiment by writing the same word or phrases with several different pens and pen nibs to find one that feels comfortable and produces an appropriate lineweight for your page. Try a variety of styles.*

❖ *Plan ahead! Always sketch out the lettering out on scrap paper before fixing it to your page. If you are going to cut the letters freehand, cut them out of scrap paper first and lay them on your page, moving them around until you find the right spot and angle.*

▲ VICTORIA, by Denise M. Johnson, Vancouver, WA. A map of the area visited makes a great background for travel photos. When you are using letters as graphic elements on a page, what they look like is as important as what they say. This bold cut-out "Victoria" announces itself in bright blue to match the background color. The cohesive page is a delightful remembrance of a colorful trip.

◀ NEW YORK CITY, by Eileen Ruscetta, Westminster, CO. For those who live in small or rural communities, a trip to the Big Apple is sure to be unforgettable. And here is yet another use of paper cutting—you can use black paper with silver and gold to create a whole skyline at night.

▶ *MANHATTAN POCKET PAGE, by Becki Spivey, Lubbock, TX. A pocket page is perfect for preserving all the memorabilia we can't seem to avoid collecting every time we travel to a new destination. Maps, brochures, and museum guides will help us remember many details we may otherwise forget over the years. Here, tucked into a half pocket on the scrapbook page, the material is actually usable. Items can be easily removed for use and then returned for safekeeping.*

▲ *NEW ORLEANS, by Trisha Wesler, King of Prussia, PA. If you didn't pick up a map of the area for your scrapbook, you can re-create the topography by making a collage of extra photographs. For this page, Trisha simply traced the outline of the state of Louisiana from an atlas and then filled in the pencil outline with photos cut to fit and arranged within the shape.*

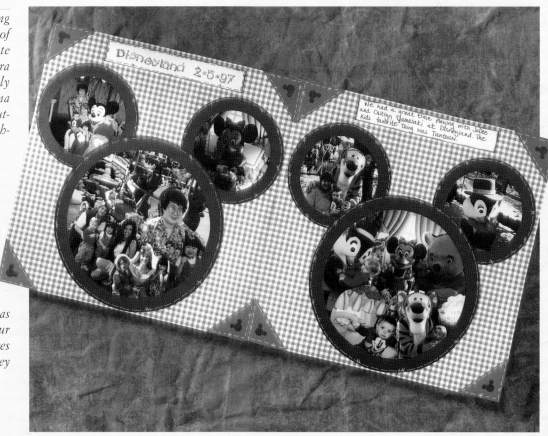

▶ *MICKEY, by Michele Robin Rank, Torrance, CA. Millions of people visit Disneyland every year, but every one of us has a unique experience and we carry away our very own memories. This simple page captures all the joy and amusement the familiar Disney characters provide.*

Clockwise from top center: Butterfly: Kathleen Paneitz, Longmont, CO. Starfish: Kathleen Paneitz, Longmont, CO, photo: Jennifer McInnes, Coarsegold, CA. Pool baby & Rose: Lorna Christensen, Covallis, OR. Ukranian festival: Gordon Gerbrandt, Broomfield, CO. Baby: Kathleen Paneitz, Longmont, CO.

Photo kaleidoscopes never fail to amaze and intrigue us, no matter how many different versions we've seen. While the technique may look difficult because of the complex-looking results, don't be intimidated. With a few good photographs and a few simple tools, such as a triangle or protractor and a craft knife, you too can create enchanting works of art. See page 46 for more information on how to design photo kaleidoscopes.

▲ *EIFFEL EMBRACE, by Gordon Gerbrandt, Denver, CO. Photograph by Deborah Mock. This is a classic twelve-piece photo kaleidoscope made from 3 1/2 x 5-inch photos using a 30-degree angle.*

▲ *VERSAILLES CHAPEL CEILING PANORAMA, by Gordon Gerbrandt, Denver, CO. Photograph by Deborah Mock. This is a classic eight-piece photo kaleidoscope made from 3 1/2 x 5-inch photos using a 45-degree angle.*

▶ *SASHA'S FAN, by Gordon Gerbrandt, Denver, CO. Photograph by Michele Gerbrandt. This clever eighteen-piece photo kaleidoscope uses eighteen photos cut with a 20-degree angle.*

▲ ORIENTAL GARDEN, *by Angela Pechin, Gilroy, CA. If you're not ready to dive into the photo kaleidoscopes described on the preceding pages, here's a technique that may warm you up to the idea. The fan used here is the perfect environment for scenic photographs of Singapore. To make a pattern, photocopy and enlarge the fan shown here to desired size. Cut the entire shape from one piece of paper, then cut two sections of a contrasting color. Crop your favorite photos to fit the fan sections. Freehand cut a tassel and attach it with drawn cords.*

TIPS FOR FOOLPROOF JOURNALING

❖ Write text freehand with a very light pencil, using a ruler for placement and alignment. Trace over the outline of the finished text with colorful pens and markers. Always use pigment-ink pens, which won't fade over time.

❖ To practice, journal on a separate piece of paper, then cut it out and mount it on the page with your photos.

❖ Use a lettering template and a light pencil to trace your writing directly onto your scrapbook page. Highlight with colorful pens and markers.

❖ Type your message on your computer using a fancy font and appropriate point size. Crop the printout, mat it, and mount it onto your page. Or trace the message onto your page using a light box.

❖ Inscribe die cuts or mats, or write around your photos in curved lines. Write inside the outline of a template, turning paragraphs into interesting shapes.

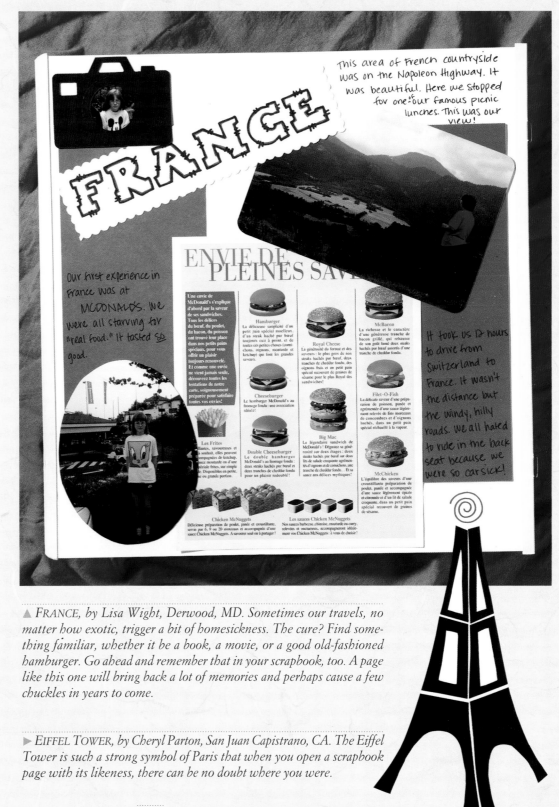

▲ FRANCE, by Lisa Wight, Derwood, MD. Sometimes our travels, no matter how exotic, trigger a bit of homesickness. The cure? Find something familiar, whether it be a book, a movie, or a good old-fashioned hamburger. Go ahead and remember that in your scrapbook, too. A page like this one will bring back a lot of memories and perhaps cause a few chuckles in years to come.

▶ EIFFEL TOWER, by Cheryl Parton, San Juan Capistrano, CA. The Eiffel Tower is such a strong symbol of Paris that when you open a scrapbook page with its likeness, there can be no doubt where you were.

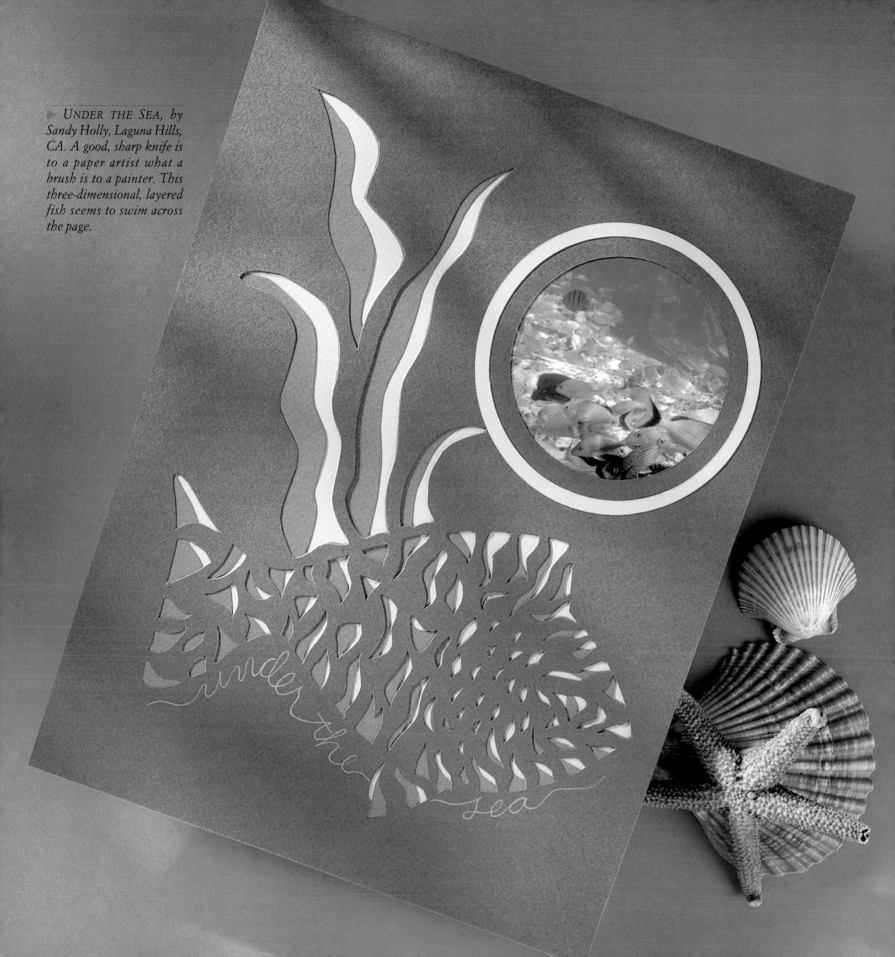

▶ UNDER THE SEA, by Sandy Holly, Laguna Hills, CA. A good, sharp knife is to a paper artist what a brush is to a painter. This three-dimensional, layered fish seems to swim across the page.

LAYERED PAPER CUTTING

Use colored paper, circle cutter or templates, cutting mat, a craft knife, stickers, and pens, and follow the steps outlined here to bring your ideas to life. A pattern for the cutout design can be sketched freehand or assembled from various commercial templates on a piece of scrap paper. Be sure to draw enough cutout sections along the outline of your design so that it can be easily distinguished.

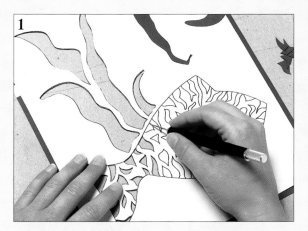

STEP 1.

Lay your page over a cutting mat. Place your pattern in the desired position. Cut out each section using your pattern as a guide. Remove the pattern and make additional cuts as desired until you are happy with the design.

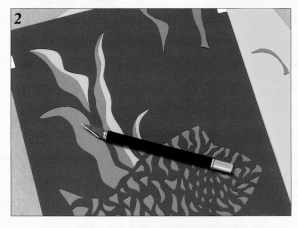

STEP 2.

Place the page over a second color of paper on top of the cutting mat. Cut out sections of the second layer as desired. The areas you cut out will reveal a third color of paper.

STEP 3.

To assemble the design, adhere the cutout page to the second cutout layer. Then adhere the second layer to a third, solid layer.

COLOR

❖ The colors in your photos will provide the information you need to choose colors for the other components of your scrapbook page—background paper, mats, and any additional decorative devices.

❖ Colors can convey different feelings or moods. Red is exciting, blue is tranquil, yellow is cheerful, green represents the "natural world." Decide what feeling or mood you want your scrapbook page to elicit in the viewer. Or what are you saying with the page? How do you feel about it?

❖ Select a color in the photo that you want to emphasize, and use shades or tones of it in the background paper, mats, and other decorative materials.

❖ Many holidays and the seasons have colors associated with them. You can play with subtle variations on the basic colors for a more unusual sophisticated look.

❖ Look at a color wheel to help you select color combinations for your scrapbook pages.

❖ Experiment by laying your photos on different color background papers to find the effect you like.

❖ Too many colors on a page is distracting.

Fall 1998 ~

THE
SEASONS

THROUGH THE YEAR

The changing of seasons creates new and fascinating photo opportunities year after year after year. When the first crocus peeks out from beneath the snow, it sets the stage for all the wonderful rites of spring that will follow. The dog days of summer are filled with baseball, lemonade stands, and stolen moments spent napping in the hammock. Autumn leaves bring us back to school or out to a tailgate party before the big football game. And winter delivers the magic of the holidays and, in the colder climates, all kinds of games to be played with the funny white stuff. Why not commemorate your favorite seasonal events in a book of their own?

Each season has its own color palette and symbols, offering excellent opportunities for creative borders and accents. A page of rust, gold, burgundy, and brown will leave no doubt about the time the page celebrates. A snowflake may be the perfect frame for your favorite winter face. The pages that follow incorporate many of our old favorite techniques along with some brand-new ones, such as the exciting paper folding technique featured on pages 98 and 99. Paper folding is another technique that may not seem natural to scrapbooking at first, but is one that opens up a fascinating world of possibilities. And what a wonderful use of those colored and printed papers .

Whatever the seasonal slant, take advantage of all the inspiration that Mother Nature and your fellow scrapbookers have to offer to create your own special book for all seasons.

▶ *GARDEN MOSAIC, by Sandra de St. Croix, St. Albert, Alberta, Canada. We've found that many scrapbookers also enjoy cooking, other crafts, and gardening as well. If you love your garden, creating a photo mosaic like this one allows you to enjoy your flowers all year long. For this effect, simply trim a photo into uniform squares and arrange the squares with a little bit of space between each one. Repeat with as many photos as will fit. This page is a reconstruction of garden scenes using one-inch squares. The finished effect is stunning.*

Heritage Trail

▲ ANNA IN BLACK AND WHITE, by Jenny Johnson, Bakersfield, CA. You can create a garden in your scrapbook even without garden photography. Just use stickers! The soft black-and-white photos are accented with colorful flower and butterfly stickers, which provide a special garden patch for Anna, who Jenny calls her "little bug."

◀ SMILING SUNSHINE BOY, by Charlotte Wilhite, Fort Worth, TX. The smile says it all here, and what better way to accentuate that warmth than with sunny printed paper? Many photographs exude a specific quality or emotion, and it's great fun to come up with a page that reflects that feeling. Here we've also used embossing powder on the corner mounts for an extra glow. Sprinkle the powder on the mounts and apply heat with a heat gun until the ink shines.

◀◀ HERITAGE TRAIL, by Janice Wiers, Merrimack, NH. Here's another type of mosaic that features scenic photographs. This page is a good way to use quite a few landscape photos and still highlight the most important subject—in this case, Benjamin. Arrange an even number of photos in a grid to cover your page, and crop your featured photo into an oval for the center. Here we've used fancy scissors and colored paper to make a mat, then we've added accents with a silver pen.

91

Small Animal Day at MSU was great. I got to hold chicks & ducks. Watched mother pig feed her babies. Holly Beers & Steve came with us.

~World of Wo

Smell Grandma's Prize Geranimums

Beep! Beep!

STEP 1.

For each full bloom, cut three colors of petals using the template we've provided. Intertwine the three petals as shown. For centers, layer silhouette flower punches cut from two different colors. Use the petal template to cut large geranium leaves from some different shades of green. For half blooms, freehand cut the petals. For the center, punch a scalloped oval and trim.

STEP 2.

For buds, punch the heart from the petal color. Punch green scalloped oval, then trim and layer as shown.

This page is finished with freehand cut stems as well as a large flowerpot and spiral punches, a rooster die cut, and lots of dots and squiggles.

◀ *WORLD OF WONDERS, by Jody Wyman, Okemos, MI. Jody's page featuring her son savoring the scent of his grandmother's prized geraniums is a delight for all three generations. And the paper geraniums that embellish the page are much quicker to make than the ones in the garden.*

FALL

Sunday, Sept. 20,98 -
Grammy, Michael & I
went apple picking.
We picked 6 apples &
ate 3. It was extremly
hot in the orchard so
we didn't stay Long.

KIMBALL
FRUIT FARM

SQUASH
EGGPLANT
PIES

© Copyright Dianne O'Hara

APPLE PICKING • RAKING

LOVE

TURKEY DINNERS

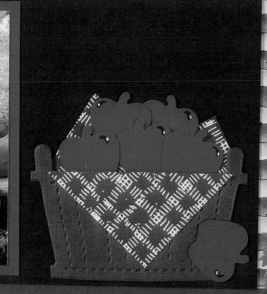

AUTUMN • HARVEST

JAKE HAD A GREAT TIME RUNNING THROUGH THE CORNFIELD AND CHOOSING HIS OWN PUMPKIN.

WE WENT TO 2 AT LOMBARD WANTED T AND WAS ABOUT

WHEN WE WENT WITH THE PRESCHOOL, THE KIDS WERE TOLD TO PICK ONE THE SIZE OF THEIR HEAD.

OCT '97   OCT '97

◄◄ (Previous spread) FALL QUILT, *by Lisa Button, Billerica, MA. Lisa sat at the dining room table thumbing through magazines looking for inspiration for a fall scrapbook page. Staring out into space, she noticed a cross-stitch sampler she had made, and that sparked the idea for this page, which won first prize in a local scrapbooking contest. Inspiration is everywhere, and there's a lot to be found in other crafts you may enjoy. Create quilt blocks of colored and printed papers and place mounted photos in the squares. Embellish your quilt with die cuts, stickers, and shapes from paper punches. You can trace things like the lettering from jam jars and other sources using a light box.*

▲ FALL, *by Charlotte Wilhite, Fort Worth, TX. Close-ups of ferns, flowers, water, gravel, bark, or cloudy skies can make strong statements when used as elements on your page. And they can set the mood or the season without detracting from your photographs. Here we've cut photos of fall leaves into one-inch strips and created a border for a two-page spread. The freehand-cut leaves used for journaling accentuate the seasonality of the page.*

◄ JAKE AND THE SCARECROW, *by Liz Kajiwara, Palmdale, CA. These pictures of Jake in a pumpkin patch leave no doubt that autumn has arrived. There are many seasonal printed papers available, such as the scarecrow paper used here, and you can use other plain and printed papers to mimic an element from your chosen paper. The pumpkins are freehand cut from a light orange paper and sponged with orange stamping ink for added dimension. Stickers and journaling complete the page.*

PAPER FOLDING

Paper folding is one of the most exciting things that ever happened to scrapbook art. With a few folds here, a few tucks there, and some creative assembly, you can frame your photos with paper art that is reminiscent of origami. And it's easy to do. There are many different folds you can use—here we present the envelope fold. By assembling folded pieces in a ring, you can create a round frame. Altering the number of folded pieces and assembly method can yield square frames, or smaller wreaths with no openings to use as embellishments. Do some experimenting. Once you start paper folding, you won't want to stop. To create the wreath shown here, you'll need twenty-five 3 x 3-inch squares of lightweight paper. Fold each piece following the instructions for the envelope fold. Try folding a practice piece first.

Paper folding technique by Kris Mason and Laura Lees.

ENVELOPE FOLD

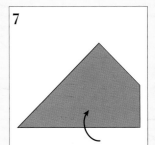

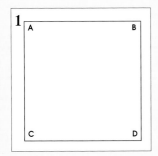

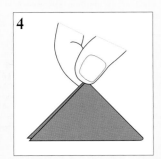

STEP 1.

Label the backside of your practice piece as shown.

STEP 2.

Fold A to D and crease the diagonal edge.

STEP 3.

Fold B to C, but do not crease the edge.

STEP 4.

Pinch the top of the triangle as shown.

STEP 5.

Unfold the square.

STEP 6.

Fold B to center pinch mark.

STEP 7.

Fold D to A.

STEP 8.

Fold C to center pinch mark.

STEP 9.

Fold C back up to E.

STEP 10.

Insert a pencil into the last fold to create a pocket.

STEP 11.

Flatten the pocket to form a small kite shape.

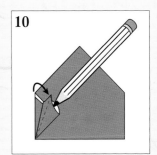

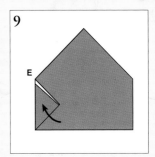

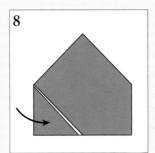

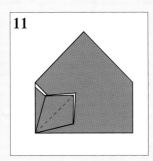

TO ASSEMBLE THE WREATH

First cut out a circle with an outer diameter of seven inches and an inner diameter of five inches (measurements will vary depending on the size of your photograph). Beginning with one folded square, "kite"-side up and point-side down, attach a small piece of double-sided tape to the front as shown. Place the next folded square on top of the one with the tape so that the bottom point of the new kite is just to the right of the previous kite. Repeat all the way around the ring, tucking the last piece under the first to finish.

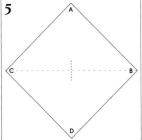

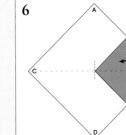

SNOWY TIMES, WARM HEARTS, by Joyce Hill Schwietzer, Greensboro, NC. Joyce and her daughter are dueling scrapbookers, working side by side. Here's what one snowy afternoon can produce. The snowflakes are cut from white cardstock with a scallop scissors. You can use the snowflakes as mats for photos or simply to embellish a page. The Christmas trees are also cut from white cardstock, and the printed paper in the background adds even more snow to the scene.

◄ ONCE UPON A SNOWY DAY, *by Joellyn Borke Johnston, Des Moines, IA. The first snowstorm in a new home adds wonder to an already wonderful time. If you're lucky and haven't packed the camera away too deep in a box, you'll be ready to capture the moment on film. Lace paper makes a textured snowy background, and the letters are cut from white paper and decorated with a snowflake stamp and ink. Punched snowflakes add the final touch.*

▲ SNOWFLAKE PICTURE FRAME, *by Pam Klassen, Denver, CO. Seize the fun of winter's first snow with a giant snowflake. The heart inset will hold six of your favorite small photos. This snowflake pattern is just one of many found in* Paper Snowflakes for All Ages *(see Sources on page 116). Use the template provided here to trace the outline of the snowflake onto your white paper. Using small scissors with sharp points, carefully cut out the silhouette and the six heart shapes. Mount small portraits behind the hearts.*

HOLIDAYS

Holidays provide wonderful material for theme scrapbooks. These special days, filled with family and friends, offer photo opportunities that only come around once a year. There are lots of holiday materials available to the scrapbook artist—stickers, printed papers, die cuts, special borders, and other seasonal decorations—making it easy to create unique pages in whatever amount of time you have available. Most holidays also have a particular color scheme, so simply using several colors of paper can set the mood.

Holidays are often full of surprises, and that's why we've included instructions in this section for creating window or lift-the-flap pages and pop-ups. Open the window of a countdown calendar or turn the page of your scrapbook to a pop-up page and discover something unexpected. We've also included a list of 25 things to do with printed paper, enough to take you through all the year's holidays and more.

When creating photographic memories of holiday gatherings, take time to write about the people, activities, or things that make this time of year special. Perhaps food is a major attraction at your get-togethers. If so, why not include recipes of traditional or your favorite dishes? Birthdays may be accompanied by gifts; consider writing a list of special presents. Whether you're celebrating one of the big holidays such as Christmas or Hanukkah, or even an esoteric one such as Groundhog Day, take the time to collect the very special memories that are so unique to these times.

▶ *CHRISTMAS TREE, by Joyce Feil, Littleton, CO. One year the Feil family made a tree-gathering journey into the forest to cut down their own Christmas tree. The whole family wandered around in the forest searching for the perfect tree. When they all agreed they had found it, all three children helped cut it down. It was the youngest child's job to yell "timber." And they remember the day in full detail whenever they look at this commemorative scrapbook page. The frame is a die cut, and the hearts are punched.*

GINGERBREAD HOUSE

For children, the weeks before Christmas can seem like an eternity, punctuated by the question, "How many days until Christmas?" A countdown calendar helps make the days fly by. Consider involving older children in creating this delightful gingerbread house, or make it for them as a surprise.

▲ *GINGERBREAD HOUSE, by Pam Klassen, Denver, CO. Bright-colored stickers adorn this holiday calendar starring Santa and Mrs. Claus centerstage. There is a lift-the-flap window to open every day from the first of December leading up to Christmas.*

TIP: MAKE IT LAST

To make your calendar more durable, use a heavy card-stock for constructing the house.

STEP 1. CUT OUT THE HOUSE

Photocopy and enlarge the house pattern on page 118. Place the pattern on brown cardstock over a cutting mat. Using a craft knife and straight edge, cut along the dotted lines through both the pattern and cardstock. Using an embossing stylus, make an indentation along the fold lines for the windows and doors. Fold open.

STEP 2. MARK AND DECORATE THE OPENINGS

Lay the cutout house on your page and lightly pencil the position of each opening. Lay the house aside. Create a scene for each window—use Christmas photos, stickers, and die cuts, or freehand-draw an object or write a message.

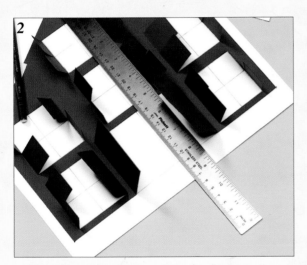

STEP 3. DECORATE THE HOUSE

Mount the house on the page, being careful to correctly position the window openings. Write the appropriate number or date on the front of each window. Decorate the gingerbread house as desired, using the example as a guide.

▲ *GLORIA POP-UP, by Erica Pierovich, Longmont, CO.*

A Pop-Up Primer

We love pop-ups. For not as much work as you might imagine, you can create a unique, special page for just the right occasion. One might think that an interactive page would have no place in a scrapbook, but that is definitely not the case. You can create marvelous pop-up pages that sit nicely in your scrapbook. The pop-up we include here offers an album spread decorated with layers of paper and die cuts along with silhouetted photos. The pop-up section is attached to the top of the page. Silhouette cut photos and follow the instructions below to create a pop-up page. Freehand cut the angel wings, harp, and trumpet.

STEP 1. CREATING THE BASE

Use a photocopier to enlarge the base pattern on page 118, or draw your own to fit your album. Cut the base from sturdy paper; fold in half, then fold flaps up. Use a straight edge to make sharp creases. If the base template is wider than your paper, cut out each side separately. Join these two pieces and reinforce the seam from behind with a one-inch strip of paper.

STEP 2. DECORATE THE BASE

Lay the pop-up base in place so you can see what parts of the page are covered or visible. Now decorate your pop-up completely, including all journaling, before mounting it on the page. For added interest, let some of the decorative elements extend above the top of the pop-up base. When decorating the center fold, leave enough "give" to allow the seam to expand and contract. Stickers do not work well. You may want to place the decorations on either side of the center fold.

STEP 3. MOUNT THE POP-UP

Position it with the center fold along the center of the gap between two pages. Close the pages to make sure the pop-up doesn't protrude outside the pages. Trim to fit if necessary.

STEP 4. ADHERE THE POP-UP

Apply two rows of adhesive to the flaps and adhere them to the pages at a 45-degree angle. The outside edges of the base will be flush at some point with the top edge of the two pages.

▲ HAPPY HANUKKAH, by Karyn Noskin, Calabasas, CA. Here's a simple way to combine many nights of celebrations onto one page. First cut candles and flames of colored paper using fancy scissors. Cut your photos to the same shape as the candles, just a bit smaller. Mount the photos and embellish the page with stickers and lettering. This idea is perfect for a holiday of several days. But it may also serve well for many other kinds of memory pages. For a totally different idea, you could use this technique to celebrate your child's birthday parties. Or early first-days-of-school.

▶ HANUKKAH COUNTDOWN, by Pam Klassen, Denver, CO. The window-a-day idea is popular with children who are anxious for the holidays to arrive. This page is constructed differently from the gingerbread house on page 104, but the effect is similar. In fact, this construction is simpler and offers an opportunity for creating with children. Cut rectangles of colored paper for the candle bases. Fold the bases in half and mount photos on the inside right of each. Mount the candles on the page, adding a freehand cut flame for each. Add freehand cut dove and Star of David, and journal a prayer or other special phrase.

▶ JELLY BEANS & EASTER EGGS, by Cindy Barents, Redlands, CA. Easter is a time for new beginnings and offers a wonderful opportunity to begin collecting family memories in a scrapbook. The egg is a great shape for creating an Easter photomontage such as the one shown here. Lightly pencil a large oval on your page, then crop and piece your photos to fit the oval. Embellish with stripes, zigzags, and diamonds cut from colored paper. The spirals, eggs, and hearts are punched, and there's always room for stickers.

◀ EASTER 97, by Trenna Hart, Kaneohe, IL. Trenna has taken the popular craft of egg painting for Easter and put it to work on this scrapbook page. Begin with egg shapes cut from plain colored or white paper and decorate the eggs with colored pencils and pens, stickers, punch art, whatever you please. Decorating paper eggs for your scrapbook is another great way to involve children in the process—just give them some paper and pencils and let them create!

25 THINGS TO DO WITH PRINTED PAPER

by Anne Wilbur

1. *Buy it. Don't stop until you have one of everything.*
2. *Organize it. File by color, pattern, or theme.*
3. *Trade it. Organize a printed paper swap meet.*
4. *Wallpaper it. Use a whole sheet as background.*
5. *Frame it. Create interesting mats for your photos.*
6. *Mat it. Choose a vivid solid color to accentuate the design.*
7. *Layer it. Create depth, dimension, and visual interest.*
8. *Coordinate it. Layer papers of similar colors and patterns.*
9. *Mix it. Break the rules and combine papers that "clash."*
10. *Match it. Choose papers with the colors of your photos.*
11. *Slice it, dice it. Cut it into strips for borders.*
12. *Weave it. Interlock strips of coordinating papers.*
13. *Stretch it. Use wider strips to create the appearance of an entire background.*
14. *Cut it, crop it. Find a die-cut machine and go to town. Or silhouette-cut printed images.*
15. *Carve it. Cut out lacy designs and lay them over a darker background.*
16. *Trim it. Use all your fancy scissors.*
17. *Tear it. Use the scraps for mosaic designs.*
18. *Punch it. Scraps are perfect for punch art.*
19. *Shape it. Cut a giant heart for a background that fills two pages.*
20. *Piece it. Use remnants to create a quilt background.*
21. *Fold it. Make pockets to keep mementos on a page.*
22. *Letter it. Trace and cut out titles for your pages.*
23. *Journal it. Hand write or use computer fonts on small-patterned papers.*
24. *Stamp, stencil, and emboss it. Great for patterned papers.*
25. *Stage it. Set up photos that will complement your papers.*

▲ SPRING HAS SPRUNG, *by Terri Fusco, Alta Loma, CA. Here's a splendid example of what printed papers can do for your scrapbook page. Combining several printed papers with various punches will add pizazz to any page. The patterned flowers and bees are created with punch art, and the green gingham mats visually tie the photos to the grass and leaves.*

Yankee

Doodle

Triston

July 4th 1998   Independence Day   I spent the holiday
playing at our home in Naperville, Illinois, with Mommy, Daddy,
twin sister Kathryn, & Auntie Leigh. It was mine & Kathryn's 21 month Birthday.

SOURCES

Suppliers

Black Ink (303) 442-5499
2300 Central Ave., Suite K
Boulder, CO 80301

C. K. Creations/CK Clips
(888) 451-8080
PO Box 21228
Bradenton, FL 34204

Carl Mfg. 847-956-0730
1862 South Elmhurst Rd.
Mount Prospect, IL 60056
(wholesale only)

Close to My Heart/D.O.T.S.
(888) 655-6552
738 E. Quality Dr.
American Fork, UT 84003

Commotion Rubber Stamps
(800) 225-4894
2711 E Elvira Rd.
Tucson, AZ 85706

Creative Express (800) 937-7686
Coluzzle®
295 W. Center St.
Provo, UT 84601

Creative Memories (800) 468-9335
P.O. Box 1839
St. Cloud, MN 56302-1839

The C-Thru Ruler Co.®
(800) 243-8419
PO Box 356
Bloomfield, CT 06002

Design Originals (800) 877-7820
2425 Cullen St.
Ft. Worth, TX 76107-1411

D.J. Inkers™ (800) 944-4680
PO Box 2462
Sandy, UT 84091

Ellison® Craft & Design
(800) 253-2238
25862 Commercentre Dr.
Lake Forest, CA 92630-8804

Family Treasures, Inc.
(800) 413-2645
24922 Anza Dr., Unit A
Valencia, CA 91355-1229

Fiskars®, Inc. (800) 950-0203
7811 W. Stewart Ave
Wausau, WI 54401

Frances Meyer, Inc.®
(800) 372-6237
PO Box 3088
Savannah, GA 31402

Geographics, Inc.
PO Box 1750
Blaine, WA 98231

The Gifted Line® (800) 533-7263
999 Canal Blvd.
Point Richmond, CA 94804

Hot Off The Press, Inc.®
(800) 227-9595
1250 NW Third Canby, OR 97013

Inspire Graphics (801) 235-9393
PO Box 935
Pleasant Grove, UT 84062

J.D. Impressions (559) 276-1633
PO Box 26895
Fresno, CA 93729-6895

Keeping Memories Alive
(800) 419-4949
PO Box 728
Spanish Fork, UT 84660-0768

Making Memories (800) 286-5263
PO Box 1188
Centerville, UT 84014
(wholesale only)

Mark Enterprises (800) 443-3430
1240 N. Red Gum
Anaheim, CA 92806

Marvy® Uchida (800) 541-5877
3535 Del Amo Blvd.
Torrance, CA 90503

Melissa Neufeld, Inc.
7068 Koll Center Pkwy. Suite 425
Pleasanton, CA 84566

Memory Makers®/Satellite Press
(800) 366-6465
475 W. 115th Ave.
Denver, CO 80234

MPR Associates®, Inc.
(800) 454-3331
PO Box 7343
High Point, NC 27264

Mrs. Grossman's Paper Co.®
(800) 457-4570
3810 Cypress Dr.
Petaluma, CA 94954-5613

The Paper Patch® (800) 397-2737
PO Box 414
Riverton, UT 84065

Pebbles in My Pocket®
(800) 438-8153
PO Box 1506
Orem, UT 84059-1506

Personal Stamp Exchange
(800) 782-6748
360 Sutton Pl.
Santa Rosa, CA 95407

Plaid Enterprises, Inc.
(770) 923-8200
PO Box 7600
Norcross, GA 30091-7600

Provo Craft (800) 937-7686
285 East, 900 South
Provo, UT 84606

SRM Press, Inc. (800) 323-9589
4216 1/2 Glencoe Ave.
Marina del Ray, CA 90292

Sonburn, Inc. (800) 527-7505
PO Box 167
Addison, TX 75001

Stickopotamus® (888) 270-4443
PO Box 1047
Clifton, NJ 07014-1047

West Trim Crafts/Memories
Forever® (818) 998-8550
9667 Canoga Ave.
Chatsworth, CA 91311

page 2
Hugs, Love, and Kisses
Printed paper–The Paper Patch
Rose Stickers–Mrs. Grossman's
Paper Co.

page 9
Daddy's Castle
Cloud paper–Frances Meyer, Inc.
Microtip scissors–Fiskars
Lettering–*Memory Makers*
Nov/Dec., 1998

page 13
Christmas Lights
Bulb clip art–D.J. Inkers

pages 14 and 15
Floral paper–Design Originals
Plaid paper–Sonburn, Inc.
*Eliza Jane Originals: Welcome the
Seasons*–Provo Craft

page 16
Rollin' Rollin' Rollin'
Printed paper–The Paper Patch
"Wow" stickers–Stickopotamus

page 19
Floral Quilt
Printed Papers–Hot Off The Press

page 22
Baby Shower
Umbrella/bear punches–Carl Mfg.
Baby carriage punch–West Trim
Crafts/Memories Forever
Heart and circle stickers–Mrs.
Grossman's Paper Co.

It's Just Intermission
Printed paper–Frances Meyer, Inc.

I Will Give Thanks Sonogram
Gingham paper–Creative
Memories
Plaid paper–Close to My
Heart/D.O.T.S.
Gold star stickers–Mrs.
Grossman's Paper Co.

page 23
Ten Tiny Fingers & Toes
Printed paper–The Paper Patch
Handprint, footprint
stickers–Frances Meyer, Inc.

pages 24–25
Caleb's Bulletin Board
Printed paper–The Paper Patch
Stamps–Close to My
Heart/D.O.T.S

page 29
A Beary Special Girl
Teddy Bear–Creative
Express/Coluzzle
Bear and border stickers–Mrs.
Grossman's Paper Co.

TEMPLATES

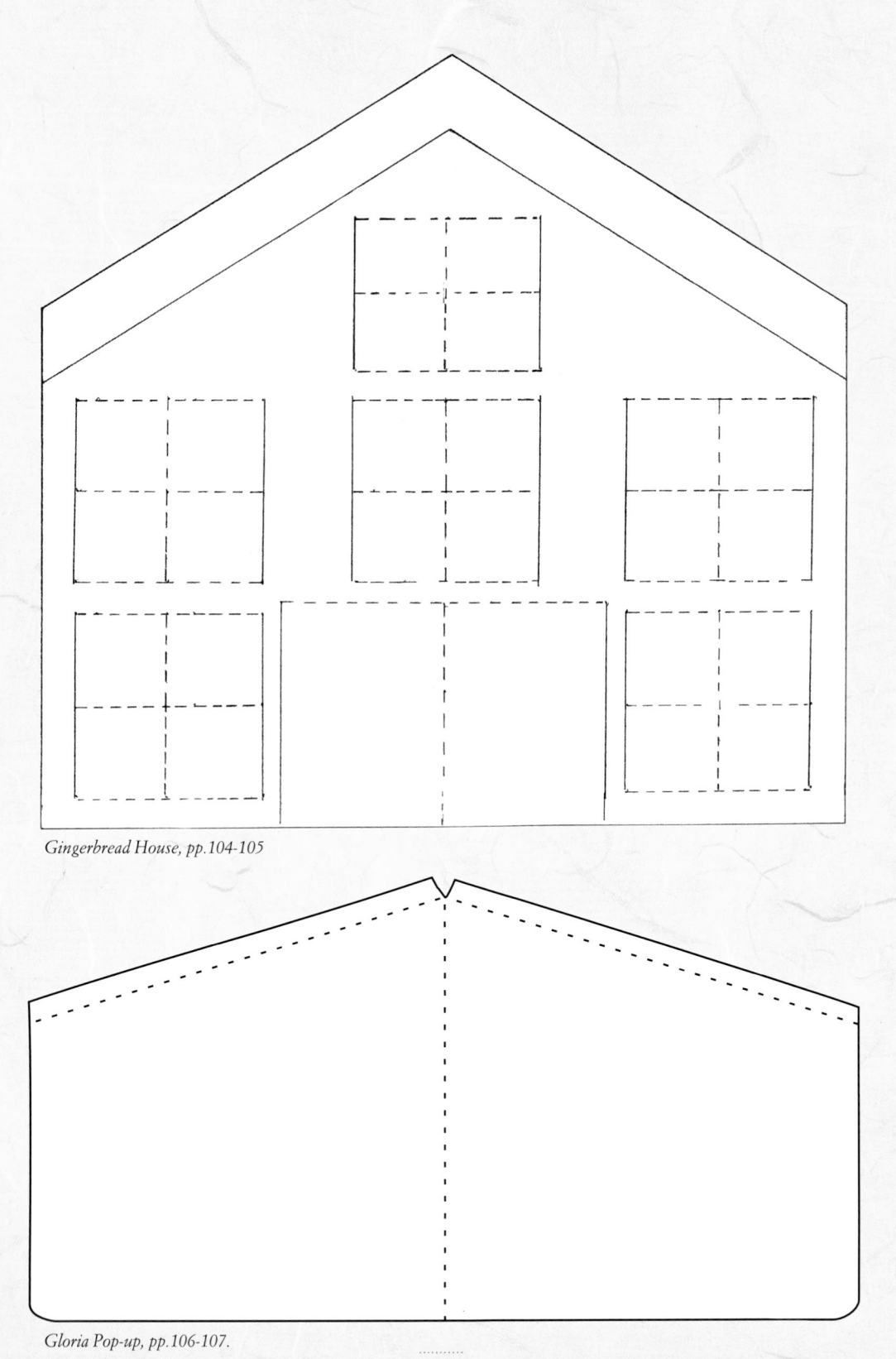

Gingerbread House, pp.104-105

Gloria Pop-up, pp.106-107.

ILLUSTRATED GLOSSARY OF TECHNIQUES

3-D PHOTOS

3-D photos can be created with two copies of the same photo. You carefully cut out the part of the photograph that you want to raise from the page, adhere it to something with a little thickness such as foam core, and place it over the same part of the other photograph copy. See p.38.

JOURNALING

Journaling is just what its name implies, writing the story of your pages in words. Journaling can be as simple as a name and/or date, or it can be a full essay of the event commemorated on your page. It can also be lyrics from a favorite song, or a poem that has special meaning for you. See pp.11, 31.

COLLAGE

Collage is a collection of different photographs pasted together on a page. The elements may or may not overlap. See p.30.

LIFT-THE-FLAPS

Lift-the-flaps pages have windows of paper that you open to reveal a photo or journaling surprise. See p.104.

FOLDED PAPER CUTTING

Folded paper cutting lets you create a perfectly symmetrical design. Fold a piece of scrap paper in half, sketch one half of the design and cut it out. When you unfold the paper, you have a symmetrical template to use on your "real" paper. See p.101.

MATTING

Matting is putting a frame of paper around your photo. You can place the photo onto a piece of paper that is the same shape but slightly larger than the image or make a cutout frame and your photograph behind it. See pp.11, 71.

CROPPING

Cropping means trimming away outside edges of your photos. Cropping is used to get rid of unwanted or unnecessary parts of the photo or to make the photo fit a particular size and shape of space. See pp.11, 38.

MONTAGE

Montage is similar to collage, but the pictures or parts of pictures are superimposed, or overlapped, so that they form a blended whole. See p.109.

EMBOSSING

Embossing involves making a paper design three-dimensional by rubbing it on a raised surface with an embossing stylus, or you can create an embossed image with embossing powder and a heat source (heat gun). See p.86.

MOSAIC

Mosaic is basically the same for the scrapbook artist as the tile artist. You cut photos into small shapes and place them on a page separated by space or a line. Photos could be cut into uniform squares and placed on a page with uniform space around each element. See p.89.

MOUNTING

Mounting simply means applying your photos or other pieces of art to your scrapbook page. See p.11.

PHOTO KALEIDOSCOPES

Photo kaleidoscopes mimic traditional kaleidoscopes. You cut an equal number of original and reversed image photos into geometric angles and piece them together. See p.46, 81.

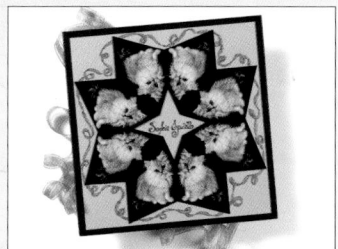

PAPER FOLDING

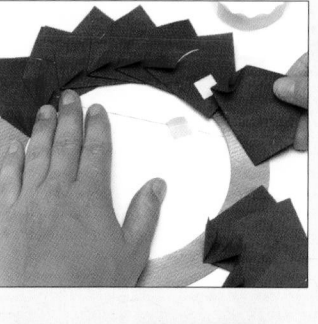

Paper folding is the art of folding paper to create designs. It involves techniques similar to origami and tea-bag folding to produce frames, borders, and embellishments for a scrapbook page. See p.28.

POP-UP

Pop-up is the art of cutting, folding and mounting so that when you open a two-page spread a design will "pop up" from the pages. See p.106.

PAPER LAYERING

Paper layering involves cutting out parts of a design to allow a different colored paper to show through. See p.84.

PUNCH ART

Punch art uses any kind of paper punched into a shape with any of the many punches made especially for this purpose. The punched-out shapes may be used as they are or folded and combined with other shapes to create a new image. See p.92.

PAPER PIECING

Paper piecing is a technique used to construct a cut paper image from various sources—punches, freehand shapes, or template designs. See p.26.

PUZZLE PAGES

A puzzle page is made by cropping photos into interlocking pieces. A Coluzzle is a template that lets you fit several photos into perfectly interlocking puzzle pieces. Coluzzle designs include a picture frame, rectangle, oval, star, heart, flowerpot, and teddy bear. See p.28.

PAPER PIERCING

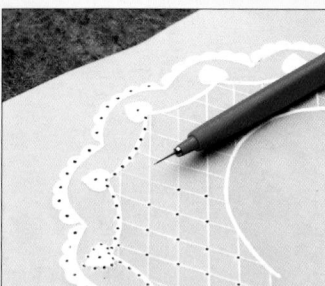

Paper piercing is a technique used to accent designs by piercing small holes in the paper. It works particularly well with parchment paper or vellum which allows the under-layering paper to show through. See p.40.

TEMPLATES

Templates are patterns used as guides in creating a drawn or cut image. See p.35.

Oh dear! What is to be the fate of little Kitty Kat!

ROCKET·LAUNCH

★ ☆ ☆ ☆ ☆ ☆ ☆

Tired of his sisters silly antics, Triston manufactured a rocket of his own design and lured her in..... trapped like a rat! He'll launch it from sea and sh.....

◄ *(Previous spread)* ROCKET LAUNCH, *by Donna W. Pittard, Kingwood, TX. Donna became a scrapbooker when her twins were born in 1996—now she fills approximately one book for each month of their lives! These July 4th pages are easy, new, and fresh. Using red, white, and blue cardstock, freehand cut shapes for rocket and sailboat. The printed "wave" paper is perfect for the water, and you can almost hear the fireworks that make the sparks of silver and white.*

▶ JACK O LANTERN, *by Dianne Gottron, Hollister, CA. With pumpkin carving and trick-or-treat costumes, Halloween presents some of the best photo opportunities. Everyone loves to see themselves dressed up, or making a mess and having a good time, and Halloween scrapbook pages are often favorites. This page uses colored paper and pens, die cuts, and a kindergarten song for journaling. The children's names are also added to the plain pumpkins.*